Words Fail

John D. Caputo, *series editor*

PERSPECTIVES IN
CONTINENTAL
PHILOSOPHY

COLBY DICKINSON

Words Fail

Theology, Poetry, and the Challenge of Representation

FORDHAM UNIVERSITY PRESS
New York ▪ 2017

Library of Congress Cataloging-in-Publication Data available online at http://catalog .loc.gov.

Printed in the United States of America

19 18 17   5 4 3 2 1

First edition

To Kristien Justaert
for all our conversations

Contents

Words Fail

Introduction

Go blind now, today:
eternity also is full of eyes—
in them
drowns what helped images down
the way they came,
in them
fades what took you out of language,
lifted you out with a gesture
which you allowed to happen like
the dance of the words made of
autumn and silk and nothingness.

—Paul Celan, from *Atemwende*[1]

In the Paul Celan poem that opens this Introduction, we witness the perpetual and yet creative tension between sight and blindness, images and darkness, gesture and language—between being removed altogether from language and being confined to its interminable oppressions. In Celan's poetry, as in so many other great poets, we enter into the ephemeral "dance of the words" that undulates like silk, but also contains the nothingness ("Nichts") that permeates our being. The initial command to "go blind" may strike us as a bit nihilistic, but it also speaks directly to the futility of using these eyes, which eternity too has in abundance, when they have witnessed an overabundance of images—including many horrific ones—passed down over the ages.

What Celan reminds us of in this haunting poem, is what his work often draws us to contemplate through his meditations on the nature of language, of the *word* itself and its harrowing passage through eternity. It is as if Celan's poetry invites us time and again to look toward the nature of language and our confinement within it in order to push its boundaries, perhaps, from time to time, to consider the possibility of a gesture *beyond* language that lifts us out of language and allows us to *happen* at all. This task, of course, would be nothing short of miraculous if brought to actual fruition. It is for this reason, I would suggest, that neither philosophy nor theology have ceased since their inception to speculate upon its potential to alter the world in which we live.

Perhaps it is the case that the only way to genuinely represent something— poetically, philosophically, politically, or even theologically—is to demonstrate one's *failure* to represent it, a claim that will bear repeating throughout this book. In this case, Celan's poetry would stand not only as a fitting testament to the failures of language but also as a prophetic witness to what such failures can gesture toward without actually presenting the "thing itself" before our very eyes. Beyond the fracturing of language through its failure to wholly capture the object it seeks to represent,[2] Celan witnesses to the poet's unique struggle against the multiple faces of oppression—the oppression of, in, and with language and the nature of representation, as well as the very literal oppressions that mar our social and political relations. What poets such as Celan, as well as his friend, Nobel Prize–winning poet Nelly Sachs, discovered in the aftermath of the World War II was that the intimate link between language and oppression was a vast and complicated one, a relationship that was often difficult to untangle within the subtle movements of fear and structural injustice where such connections were often formed.

This book, in short, is concerned with these matters of representation and failure, especially insofar as they indicate deep and often startling truths about the nature of spiritual and theological reflection. I turn to poets such as Celan, Wallace Stevens, Adrienne Rich, Giovanni Pascoli, and Giorgio Caproni because they are all poets who sought directly to enter into the struggle with oppression that takes place within language. In this manner, they thereby illuminate the tensions present within the failures of representation in a rather profound manner, the very thing I wish to highlight as we progress through the narrative I construct. Since this was their chosen task, and though formulated in a variety of ways, each poet maintained an almost singular quest to demonstrate the power of poetry in unlocking the "thing itself" beyond the various linguistic, social, historical, cultural, or religious representations that seemingly confined it—even if such an exposure was possible only in the thing's failure to be represented.

The journey on which this study of poetic struggle against oppression and representation has taken me has been one that has seen this particular effort linked with various contemporary continental thinkers whose work has continued to highlight the vast philosophical and theological stakes at play within these poetic endeavors. There has been much philosophical speculation on the potential failure of language as well as the search for a presentation of the "thing itself" beyond representation. Here, accordingly, I pursue the writings of a trio of philosophers—Jacques Derrida, Philippe Lacoue-Labarthe and Giorgio Agamben—as prime examples of how modern poetry presents us with a profitable vantage point from which to survey these ongoing struggles of living in a highly fragmented (post)modern world.

As I pursued these intersecting lines of inquiry in terms of poetics, I also began to notice that, despite each thinker's desire to address questions of religious identity, little work had actually been done to look specifically at the form of spirituality that is given shape by this intersecting of poetics and theological-philosophical reflection. Yet, just such a focal point was beginning to take shape in my reflections on how their understanding of poetics and religious identity were offering rich suggestions about our spiritual nature. Studies such as these are highly invested in the potentiality of the human subject, something that continuously evokes an aura of spirituality as it is made manifest within our being. Having already taken some time elsewhere to outline Agamben's elaboration of potentiality upon theology as a whole,[3] I investigate the implications that a turn to potentiality holds for the development of a form of spirituality that is perhaps atheological in some sense, but, for that very reason, capable of reformulating what we consider spirituality, and therefore theology as well, to be in the first place. My selection of authors is certainly geared toward opening up such a discussion that much wider, with the hope, in the end, of providing something of a platform for the ceaseless (self-)critique of philosophical, theological, and poetic structures within both thought and experience.

With this goal in mind, it was from the outset of the composition of the present work that I began to ask myself some very pointed questions that would push me along this path of inquiry: What does theology have to learn from an investigation on the interplay between presentation and representation, and the quest to express anything at all in language? What does the formulation of a spirituality in light of these authors' takes on the nature of language and potentiality likewise say about the act or art of writing, and the deep wellspring of potential that can be accessed in it, even for writers themselves? These questions, I felt, may shed a good deal of light on the poetic process itself which many poets have undergone, as well as those seeking to disseminate their experiences into fields other than poetry. Furthermore, I wondered, how might such a state of linguistic "failure"—something that can perhaps be described as an atheological movement, as Agamben himself will do—actually put us in touch with an endless source of spiritual and creative potential? And how can an experience of this potential provide us with an entirely new way of perceiving our role within language and, more specifically, our role as writers who struggle a good deal to present our thoughts and even our very selves within words? The book accordingly follows this trajectory of thought very closely, meandering through a variety of thinkers and poets in order to conclude in the Conclusion with a more original exposition of the process of writing (and even publishing) in a contemporary context.

In chapter 1, I explore the French thinker Jacques Derrida's rich reworking of the Kantian regulative principle of the *as if* in order to point toward certain potential movements of the *as such* in the poetry of Wallace Stevens, Adrienne Rich, and Paul Celan, as well as the various mystical traditions that Derrida himself took up on occasion. Fundamentally, the *as if* is as much about faith as it is about politics insofar as it requires people to believe in a given representation—*as if* it were really *as such*—in order to establish the normative boundaries that identify persons and grant us some sense of cultural intelligibility as it were. Hence, the borders between genders, races, and cultures appear as (contested) sites of belief, as do the borders that are said to exist between humans and animals or humans and the divine. By taking this precise path and yet staying open to Derrida's critique of any possible presentation *as such* beyond the *as if*, I hope to show how Derrida's work ultimately also points toward an encounter with the other *as such*, beyond the *as if*, though within language, very much within its failures—which is, in the end, the only real way to fully respect the encounter at all. In such fashion, an ethical imperative appears within the event of encounter, one that does not seek to reduce the singularity of the other's presence before us to a regulative ideal as if to go beyond what has been (re)presented to us, but rather that which embraces what *cannot* be represented, bringing philosophy, politics, and religion to the threshold of a mystical-ethical imperative that we must take very seriously.

Chapter 2 attends more directly to the legacy of Celan's poetry as his work is critiqued and appropriated by both Derrida and Philippe Lacoue-Labarthe—two thinkers whose studies of Celan have become essential reading for comprehending the nature of his poetics. Here I try to disentangle their uses of Celan in order to locate a hope for new subjectivities in the face of the repeated failures of language and artistic representations alike. What I try to make clear throughout my analysis is that both thinkers, in their varied efforts to use Celan's work to distinguish between poetic representation and the possibility of a presentation beyond representation, open us up to new ways to think about faith in a modern, and very fragmented world. In this way, the concept of failure moves to the center stage of this book, and assists us in comprehending why our failures to genuinely represent anything (i.e., ourselves, others, the divine, etc.) may be the only possible way that we can convey an authentic presence. At the same time, this insight also begins to reformulate the terms upon which we have traditionally understood religious thought and identity. At this point, I bring in the work of the American poet Adrienne Rich in order to somewhat illuminate the directions in which poetry and faith might possibly be headed as they also intersect and interweave with one another, the very coordinates of the "theo-poetic" that has gained so much currency as of late.

Chapter 3, in many ways, extends this trajectory of thought into a dialogue with the work of the Italian theorist Giorgio Agamben. Despite the growing popularity that Agamben's work is currently experiencing, there is little critical material available that would seek to unite his earlier, more literary work with his later philosophical, political, and theological ruminations, such as those centered on the figure of the *homo sacer*, the Western legacy of the messianic, the called-for forces of profanation or his development of an ontology of pure potentiality. Lacking this connection, I believe an opportunity is missed, not only to illuminate the overall unity of Agamben's thought, but also to more fully develop a radical conception of poetics today in relation to the philosophical, *as well as* the theological. Beginning with his characterization of a *scission* within language that posits *philosophy* as that which can know its object without possessing it and *poetry* as that which can possess it without knowing it, I demonstrate how his earlier work on poetry maintains a necessary correlation with his later philosophical and theopolitical writings. In this context, I explore his development of a poetic atheology that is a sort of materialist metaphysics, the potential last refuge of meaning in an otherwise nihilistic world—one that contains dire implications for the fields of poetry, philosophy, and theology. Although the establishment of poetry as a last refuge of meaning over and against the destruction of experience in the modern era is a bold claim to be sure, I think it expresses Agamben's attempt to reformulate the possibility for meaning to emerge beyond its inscription in language, as well as the conditions under which theology could be understood as a profane endeavor that tries to speak to this situation of human existence—a connection I hope to clarify a good deal in what follows.

The conclusion, to my mind, encapsulates everything that has come before it, but also concretizes the theoretical advancement into new territory, allowing me to utilize a more creative approach to summarizing and synthesizing the main points made throughout the first three chapters. Rather than such a conclusion being out of sync with what comes before it, I rather read this "final chapter" as an alternate, and somewhat more original account of what the book's aims are—one more readable in many ways and synthetic in its incorporation of others' valuable insights. In other words, there would be no conclusion such as the one presented here without the hard work of the first three chapters. Its focal point is accordingly to be found in the development of a material spirituality lodged within the potentiality of the human being—something that need never be severed from the possibility of encounter with an other, even if such an encounter continuously fails to be recorded in words—and which I examine here through the concrete dynamics found in the practices of writing and publishing. Though this may seem in many ways to be a departure from the analysis of poetics and faith that defines the rest of the work, it is my hope that the astute reader will comprehend that what I am suggesting in the conclusion is rather a creative summation and original synthesis of the implications that have preceded it. Though the conclusion could certainly stand alone from the rest of the work, I believe that it will only achieve its fuller sense in light of what came before it, and, in this sense, it can point us beyond the merely theoretical and toward that creative and spiritual dimension of human existence we have been pining for all along, that which pushes the boundaries of both philosophy and theology more than just a little bit, and which may only be graspable *through* the failures of our representations.

The Logic of the "As If" and the (Non)existence of God
An Inquiry into the Nature of Belief

As if, as if, as if the disparate halves
Of things were waiting in a betrothal known
To none, awaiting espousal to the sound

Of right joining, a music of ideas, the burning
And breeding and bearing birth of harmony,
The final relation, the marriage of the rest.
                    —**Wallace Stevens, "Study of Images II"**[1]

Dwelling on the image, the very essence and form of representation, the American poet Wallace Stevens once contemplated a sense of harmony long sought after as a sort of completion of images. They *are* images that cannot fade in his estimation because they "are all we have," as he states earlier in the poem "Study of Images I"—they "can be no more faded than ourselves." Yet they can, of course, be false in some sense as well—a "stale" desire that strives toward a harmony seemingly forever suspended by the thrice repeated conditional nature of the "as if" which accompanies it in this particular poetic speculation.

Following the stories of Greek mythology, as Stevens here does, it is the marriage of Mars and Venus that brings about the birth of *Harmonia* (in Greek) or *Concord* (in Latin), a marital unity that he invokes directly in his two-part poem "Study of Images." This is a title that itself seems to convey the significance of the subject that Stevens is attempting to circumscribe. The perpetual oppositions between war and love, sun and moon, male and female, as between Mars and Venus, are brought to a harmonious *concord*, we might say, one that indicates, for Stevens, the tensions present within the realm of representations or images as a whole. If understood this way, we live always poised to realize a unity that never seems to come, that is truly, as Stevens suggests, "known to none." It is always "as if, as if, as if" it were about to happen, though it never actually comes to pass. As Stevens's poem seeks to demonstrate, this is perhaps the great truth that undergirds humanity's quest for constructing images, something repeatedly sought after in the poetic endeavor to present things as they are (as such)—though it is more likely to be achievable, if at all, we might say, in the conditional nature of the "as if." The relationship between these two seemingly conflicted poles (the "as such" and the "as if") will in fact come to generate the entirety of what we might call the hermeneutical field of representations—political, social, religious or otherwise.

For its part, Greek mythology, as one might suggest is typically the case, manages to give symbolic, narrative form to the underlying truths of our need for constructing images or representations. If we follow further the genealogy that Stevens explores, we are led to note that Harmonia, the daughter of Mars and Venus, later married Cadmus, the legendary founder of Thebes and the figure whom Herodotus credited as having brought the alphabet to Greece. Their union in turn produced a child, Semele, the eventual mother (along with the father, Zeus) of the young god Dionysus. This, at least, is the version of events which Euripides relates to us in his play *The Bacchae*, a drama centered on the arrival of this relatively new god into the Greek pantheon of deities.[2]

In the course of time, however, the plot comes to center upon King Pentheus, grandson of Cadmus by another daughter. He is, in his essential role within the play, a king who emphatically denies the existence of the young god Dionysius and forbids any worship of him, considering him to be outside the laws of the city of Thebes. It is this series of events— the presentation of a new deity alongside a denial of him by the ruling sovereign—that is not far removed from the suspended (conditional) nature of harmony that Stevens invoked in "Study of Images II." Rather, the "as if" comes to dominate Euripides's all-too-brief meditations on the nature of belief as well, something that comes to a head in a scene that highlights the aporias of representation (of dwelling within its laws).

In this particular scene from *The Bacchae*, Cadmus, the father of Semele and the husband of Harmonia, speaks to Pentheus and attempts to convince him of the apparent necessity for believing Dionysus to be a god. Indeed, the inclusion of a deity into the familial clan would bring great honor to the family and could perhaps even serve to eradicate the social shame they have already incurred. What is of great interest here is the manner in which belief, in a very literal sense, is linked by Cadmus to a state of dwelling within the laws, or *nomoi*, of communal life, whether they be societal or familial. This is the case despite the fact that the worship of Dionysus is currently considered outside the laws, or prescribed norms, of the city. As Euripides depicts the scene at this point:

> My son, Tiresias exhorted you well;
> dwell with us, not outside ["in the wilderness beyond"] the accustomed
>   ways [*nomoi*, laws].
> For at present your mind has taken wing, and your thought is no thought.
> Even if this is no god, as you assert,
> let him be called one by you—tell a lie in good cause ["declare well and
>   falsely"],
> that he is Semele's child, so that it may seem that she bore a god
> and we gain honour for all our family.[3]

Semele was the mother of Dionysus by Zeus, as I have already indicated, a truth that no one believed and which was the source of her dishonor shortly before her sudden death brought about through viewing the radiant fullness of her lover's being. Pentheus, however, is here advised by Cadmus, her father, to accept the god *as if* he were real, false though this act may be, a point that even Cadmus acknowledges may be the case. This is yet an act, we are told, that would render him capable of dwelling with, and *within*, the laws of the family—*the* significant effect to achieve. It would be a disingenuous act, to be sure, but all semblance of belief would be maintained and the social standing of the family might, as such, increase. Real belief, Cadmus seems to be saying, comes second, if at all, to its cultural representation.

It is intriguing, then, that law (*nomoi*) should figure here so prominently in Euripides's play, at least insofar as Dionysus is deemed to be "outside" the laws of the polis—just as his female worshippers leapt and danced themselves into a divine frenzy on the outskirts of the city. In this light, Cadmus's exhortation made to Pentheus to return within the laws (of the clan, or of the family) takes on a new meaning, as the laws of belief in this deity are outside the laws of the polis yet they do adhere to an apparent rule or norm of another community. As Charles Segal has hinted, perhaps the conflict of laws within this context is indicative of another tension, one of symbolic meaning in general.[4] Seen this way, the conflict of symbols that Euripides confronts cannot be entirely held together and causes him to seek new forms of language that attempt to go beyond the familiar structures of language's everyday usage.[5] The play thereby confronts the warring poles of the rational (*logos*) and the irrational (*mythos*) for which there was no apparent mediation.[6] Euripides's tragedy, like all tragic art, tries to

hold these irresolvable tensions between, what Segal calls, the "centrifu-
gal" and "centripetal" forces it contains, those forces that tend toward chaos
and those that tend toward order.[7] Hence, tragedy, as the work of art that
brings order to our chaotic world, is capable of shaping nature into an intelligible form, but also, it would seem, of shaping our belief in these systems
of order that circulate as so many laws in our world.

In short, what Euripides confronts us with in the course of this highly
revealing scene is the essential dilemma of faith given over to a contemplation of the nature of representation as a whole, a dilemma that has not become less problematic over the course of time. The sought-after images in
which we seek to identify ourselves and, in turn, in which we are identified—
whatever their social nature—must seemingly be upheld as the very basis
for cultural intelligibility, no matter the falsity of their nature, or so Cadmus's position would have us believe. Some, therefore, even today, are, like
Cadmus, who had joined himself to Harmonia, given over to belief in what
may be false so that appearances (equated by Euripides with law, *nomoi*)
that give order (*harmony, concord*) to society might be maintained. That is,
many make an attempt to dwell in semblances *as if* they were genuine so
that the traditional structures of representation might hold and so that society might hold together with them. The conditions of intelligibility, such an
intention suggests, depend upon just such an accord being struck. Some,
like Pentheus, however, refuse to cooperate with this patently falsified
scheme, becoming, in fact, the "unbelievers" who threaten the workings of
the system and are seemingly destroyed by their unwillingness to engage
in these fabricated images. In many ways, this is perhaps an expression of
the preference to live under another law (than the polis's law) and the
clash of representations and cultures that we so often encounter in our
world. (Pentheus, in fact, at play's end, is torn limb from limb by the fren-
zied female worshippers of Dionysus. A tragic ending for one who was not
able to *see* the necessity of believing in a deity he could not be certain of.)
Yet others, like Cadmus's daughter Semele, yearn to glimpse what lies
wholly beyond representation, or that which cannot be fully absorbed by
a finite creature, to view the absolute overwhelming pureness of an exposed
divinity and so perish in full view of what can never be expressed by human
beings in language or symbol.

There is genuinely little that has been subsequently added to this lengthiest tale of how history has attempted to grapple with the representations
that structure and give meaning to our world. It is a struggle also, I would
suggest, perhaps best expressed through the conditionality of the "as if,"
which both Stevens and Euripides place right before our eyes, and, yet it
is that of which we have such difficulty comprehending its nature and func-

like yHlwH
in OT, too

tion. From this point of view, representation becomes a regulative principle that seems to hold a fundamental place in describing the (often unexpressed or unknown) hopes pinned upon our construction and use of images. It is, as the history of thought has already witnessed, the lynchpin of belief itself, perhaps best embodied in the problematic surrounding the origin and lineage of a conjecture on belief like Pascal's wager. For Pascal, we would do well to recall, the wager to be made upon God's existence was in essence a bid to create belief within an individual's heart simply by weighing the merits of believing in the divine, and then pronouncing this belief as a quasi-certitude grounded upon the conditional "as if": as if simply believing *as if* there were a god were enough to guarantee some sort of validity to the claim itself.[8] What Pascal repeats, of course, without saying as much, is Cadmus's attempt to stay within the *nomoi* of traditional representational limitations without actually contesting their content. Pascal's wager, however, might be more convincingly portrayed as itself an attempt simply to provide verification that there is a crack within the representational logics at work in our world. These logics, as even Cadmus would admit, are rendered futile in their efforts to establish that a god (*must* or *should*) exist, though they are also logics that have traditionally been filled with the presumed existence of the divine—the ultimate guarantor of all representations taken as being a part of nature.

In this context perhaps as modern as ancient, we certainly enter into the varied historical musings of an otherwise overlabored ontotheology. Traditional proofs for God's existence, from this viewpoint, could be portrayed as little more than so many attempts to resolve the irresolvable aporias present within human experience, and this might explain why trying to prove God's existence has fallen so far out of favor today. In other words, what Pascal seems to be doing is little more than suggesting the necessary existence of "as if" statements themselves, truly, in fact, saying nothing about the potential existence or nonexistence of an actual divine being. What this analysis points to, instead of guaranteeing the existence of God, is that a fundamental (mis)reading of the nature of the "as if" has dominated the history of ontotheological speculation, from the earliest Greek mythologies to the present day—and it is *this* legacy that we are still needing to take up within the present moment.

The essential nature of the "as if," I would assert, remains a major unresolved problematic with which neither philosophy nor theology has adequately dealt. In what follows, I will demonstrate, however, that a particular Kantian appropriation of the "as if" (*als ob*), as developed in the work of Jacques Derrida, may hold a key to a contemporary understanding of the necessity of the conditional, formulated in his work most directly as the desire for the poetic as such over and beyond—though in some sense also dependent upon—the religious "as if." Moving along these lines, I want to delve into this matter in order to demonstrate how altering our perspective on the nature of representations can open us up, not simply to new forms of representation, but to new ways of relating to the representations already before us—providing a new and paradoxically dwelling material spirituality.)

The Philosophical Nature of the "As If"

It would be quite problematic to try to distinguish the conjectural, conditional claims for divine existence made by both Euripides and Pascal from Kant's positing of the existence of God as based upon a similar "as if" model of thought, for all three share in a seemingly profound overlap of interests. In what has become, in many ways, the historical centerpiece of philosophical reflections upon the nature of the "as if," Kant's claim that God's existence must be assumed as morally necessary has come to dominate subsequent thoughts upon the nature of belief itself. In his second *Critique*, for example, God's existence is something we must "assume," Kant tells us, as it can only be based on the possibility of the highest good being transformed into a reality.[9] And, as he states elsewhere:

> One cannot provide objective reality for any theoretical idea, or prove it, except for the idea of freedom, because this is the condition of the moral law, whose reality is an axiom. The reality of the idea of God can only be proved by means of this idea, and hence only with a practical purpose, i.e., to act as though (*als ob*, "as if") there is a God, and hence only for this purpose.[10]

In terms of the Kantian "regulative principle" (formulated in relation, he stresses, to "all cosmological ideas"), which is most fully developed in the first *Critique*, there is "no experience of an absolute boundary" in empirical terms when one considers cosmological questions. Hence, there is "no experience of a condition as one that is absolutely unconditioned empirically."[11] The conditional is all that truly remains—a fact to which later interpreters, such as Derrida, as we shall see, cling fast. This logic would encompass the existence of God as well, an idea that could never be validated as a concrete, empirical reality.[12] The unconditional is all that can finally be asserted as indicative of an otherwise inevitable "regress to infinity" that Kant discerns at work in our general schemes of representation.

In "On the final aim of the natural dialectic of human reason" of the second *Critique*, Kant resolutely maneuvers his analysis of the problematic of universals and the nature of representation as a whole under the auspices of the "as if" (*als ob*). It is the "as if" which actually allows reason to comprehend "the possibility of things in the world of sense."[13] In so many words, everything in Kant's discernment of universals seems to lie within the realm of the "as if," which makes Kant's ethics, as well as any positing of the existence of God, sustainable. In the end, some form of deism is all that philosophy could potentially justify, though even this claim is ultimately without any empirical verification.[14] Like Pascal, Kant's determination of God's existence seems rather to point toward the fractured nature of representation itself, something that will continue to haunt any proofs waiting to be given for God's existence.

Despite any neo-Kantian attempts to develop an ethics of the "as if" upon these basic principles, his ethics is ultimately founded upon a conjecture, to act *as if* there were a God, which is, for some, perhaps to do away with God practically speaking.[15] Such a position is lurking in what Richard Kearney has more recently attempted to discern through distinguishing between the function of the analogical "as" and the fictive "as if." Narrative wagers, the stuff of religious scripture, according to Kearney, are more about "imagination and hospitality" than about "calculation and blind leaps." Specifically, in contrast to Pascal's wager, he tells us, "they solicit fidelity not fideism."[16] He goes on to state that the "as if" can only ever be a fictive proposition, whereas the "as" itself is an analogical attempt to state truth (e.g., "the stranger *as* divine").[17] For him, a belief that he calls "anatheism" is about a forward-looking repetition, and, through this gesture, a return to the divine via the analogical "as." The stranger, if taken *as* divine, would allow a concrete presence to unfold before us, whereas, the fictive "as if" suspends our belief entirely, never really to return. It is the alliance between atheism and theism that signals a sort of "post-theism" for Kearney, a belief in a God who *may be*—what, in reality, may be the only truthful way to discuss the existence of God.[18] In this way, he faults contemporary poststructuralists such as Derrida (whose own position on the "as if" will be taken up shortly), for not returning to any (narrated) sense of divinity (a named God) in their writings, leaving faith ultimately suspended and without resolution, without a concrete force appearing before us.[19] In essence, Kearney finds them lacking the finesse of an anatheistic (hermeneutic) response, which he intends to further draw out in his own work.

Kearney's critique would seem, in so many words, to be aimed directly at those Kantian reductions of narrative identities which would efface any particularity of the divine in favor of a generalized (perhaps even vague) deism, or atheism. Despite his criticisms, however, Kearney's objections appear to struggle somewhat in their making a definitive distinction between a Pascalian wager in a God who might or might not exist and Kearney's emphasis upon a God who may be, perhaps in the end (and for the same reasons that we will see at work in Derrida's thought) because there is a fundamental indeterminacy at play within any determination (*as* a representation), one that harbors a vast potential to unlock our (theo) poetic imaginative, and narrative, landscape. This is to say that despite our ability to treat the stranger *as* divine, this gesture of hospitality says nothing about the actual (non)existence of the divine, only the nature of our hospitable act.

To develop a representation of God, or of anything, the "as if" will, in some sense, still have to be utilized, even if we wish to treat one thing potentially *as* another. Indeed, to treat even a stranger *as* divine, we would first have to utilize something like the "as if" (as a regulative principle) to formulate what our notion of divinity would be in the first place (i.e., that it is to be welcomed, treated as good, etc.). In this sense, Kant's influence continues to move through the modern history of philosophical reflection upon the nature of universals and the regulative principles of thought, despite Kearney's possible objections. From this viewpoint, the "as if" has not gone away, but has actually become solidified as the paradoxical (*aporetic*) essence of what constitutes any representational identity, and, in general, of what constitutes any attempt to formulate *belief* itself.

The influence of Kant upon Derrida's work, for example, has continued to outline such a reading.[20] This should come as little surprise to Derrida's close readers, though it does seem to provide an immediate clash of sorts as the great systematic regulator of thought is aligned with the "father of deconstructionism." It is hardly a profound observation, however, that Derrida's writing was dependent upon the strategic usage of conditional (*if* or *as if*) statements, something that lay at the foundations of all of Kant's systematic reflections, as we have just seen. This is so because Derrida's rhetoric was itself dependent upon a state of undecidability that ran as a current throughout his entire oeuvre, though this is not to suggest that Derrida and Kant overlap entirely on their use of conditional statements.[21]

In general, I find Hager Weslati's analysis of the "as if" to be quite accurate: Derrida's use of the "as if" is a force of dissemination and expansion ("an essential component of 'différance'"), in contrast to Kant's usage, which, for its part, was an attempt to provide a foundation for metaphysics and to bridge the gaps within experience.[22] Despite this nuance, however, Derrida's use of the "as if" does essentially conform to the Kantian notion of its being a "regulative idea," as a preservation of the necessity for representation itself (i.e., "there is nothing outside the text"). This is perhaps also why, in so many words, Derrida's comments on experience are seemingly so often removed from being indebted to particular, concrete traditions, heritages, canons, or religions.[23] It is the universal structure of experience, once so important to Kant, that Derrida must engage if representations— themselves posited as intelligible only through the use of the "as if"—are to continue to have any meaning.

In a short article on rogue states that later became part of his book *Rogues: Two Essays on Reason*, for example, Derrida unfolds his indebtedness to the Kantian "regulative idea" which is mired in the use of the "as if."[24] In this fashion, the "decisive and enigmatic role played by the *als ob* in all of Kant's thought" comes back to Derrida as a central principle within his own work. As he suggests:

> [I]f we come back this time to the strict meaning Kant gave to the *regulative* use of ideas (as opposed to their *constitutive* use), we would, in all rigor, and in order to say anything on this subject, and especially in order to appropriate such terms, have to subscribe to the entire Kantian architectonic and critique, something I cannot seriously undertake or even commit myself to doing here. We would have to begin by asking about what Kant calls "the different interest in reason" (*ein verschiedenes Interesse der Vernunft*), the *imaginary* (the *focus imaginarius*, that point toward which all the lines directing the rules of understanding—which is not reason—tend and converge and thus indefinitely *approximate*), the necessary *illusion*, which need not necessarily deceive us, the figure of an approach or approximation (*zu nähern*) that tends indefinitely toward rules of universality, and especially the indispensable use of the *as if* (*als ob*). . . . We cannot treat this here, but I thought it necessary at least to note, in principle, how circumspect I would be to appropriate in any rigorous way this idea of a "regulative Idea."[25]

Here, the problematic nature of the "as if" within all representational logics is best understood as essentially bound to the tendencies toward universalization, part and parcel of the imaginary, the "necessary illusion, which need not necessarily deceive us." Though this is a very limited and wary taking up of the conditional thematic within Kant's work, Derrida is far from finished with his confrontation with the "as if." Indeed, as I intend to show, the "as if" almost becomes *the* principle by which to grasp his reflections upon representation, reason, metaphysics, and belief, not to mention the intriguing and often enigmatic suggestions he made over the years concerning his relationship to historical religious traditions, especially his own Judaic heritage.

As I will argue, Derrida's dealings with the "as if" are firmly entrenched within its historical disclosure as a principle indissociable from all attempts at forming culturally intelligible representations. Hence, this "necessary illusion" of the "as if" appears as the revealed structure of representation, something Derrida must speak of openly so as not to deceive us, so as not to do violence to us through any hidden or obscured (ontotheological) illusions. His characterizations of justice and of responsibility that run as a single thread throughout much of his later work would seem to dictate nothing less than this willingness. These are "necessary illusions" that are essential to all acts of representation and that are rendered "less violent" through their more or less being exposed as the illusions they are, hence as not necessarily deceptive. They are, as Derrida seems to indicate above, only an "approximation." Yet, they are also what Cadmus once asked Pentheus to declare his loyalty to, though falsely, so that the laws of society might be further upheld. They are, in this manner, to be completely opened to their subsequent deconstruction.

It is this tension of living within a "necessary illusion" which does "not necessarily deceive us" that in turn comes to generate a specific conception of history for Derrida, as well as those religious and philosophical markers of our traditional identities, something he posits as ranging all the way back to Platonism and its subsequent reliance upon the representative image. If this lineage between "us moderns" and the Judaic and Greek takes on representation seems somewhat arbitrary, it is nonetheless fundamental for Derrida: "Are we Jews? Are we Greeks? We live in the difference between the Jew and the Greek, which is perhaps the unity of what is called history."[26]

Taking our point of departure from Greek thought is therefore no coincidental or arbitrary starting point, for such is his pronouncement in an essay devoted to underscoring the nature of how violence and metaphysics interact. His concluding reference to the Joycean "jewgreek" or "greekjew" that identifies all of us, would only seem to further cement the impossibility of ever fully appropriating any particular, historical religious identification. Rather, we are always caught in a suspension between the tensions of representation, much as Euripides had tried to illustrate through his pushing of language to its boundaries.[27] It is not a stretch to see how these formulations, as we will see in a moment, lead him to identify the regulative structure of the "as if" with the "relation without relation" that is characteristic of his many similar Levinasian universalizations[28]—how indeed a "religion without religion" could be said to spring from this conditional site.

What Remains of Derrida's Faith

Derrida's relationship to religious thought has frequently been opened to multiple (mis)readings, from Judaic to Christian to atheistic.[29] To give but one recent example of how problematic this discourse on Derrida's religious (non)affiliations has been, we would do well to note how Leonard Lawlor, in a series of lectures devoted to Derrida's work on animality, struggled himself with identifying Derrida's religious strands of thought. For Lawlor, it is Derrida's insistence upon a "weak force" moving through history that is "one of the voices of Christianity" that influences his work. Yet Derrida also, Lawlor tells us, attempts to point beyond Christianity, through a deconstruction of Christianity, to a space prior to Christianity and, therefore, he is not to be considered a Christian.[30] The paradoxical logic of "belonging without belonging" that Derrida famously appropriated from the work of Levinas—and that came to dominate his later thoughts on concrete, historical institutions—is on full display once again in Lawlor's formulations, though it seems also to be very much applicable to a variety of religious traditions and histories.

As I have already been suggesting throughout, what we are, in truth, dealing with in Derrida's conceptualization of religious identity is the nature of representation itself, the manner in which *any* person could be said to identify with *any* particular religious heritage. To see things as such is, at once, an expansion of the Kantian "regulative idea" best exemplified in the workings of the "as if," though it is also a restriction of its operations, a movement away from utilizing the conditional as a "filler of the (metaphysical) gaps" (thus being utilized to posit God's existence, for example) and toward its being embraced as the "condition without condition" that grounds every reflective operation. Religion, in this sense, seems only at times to be an emblematic figure within Derrida's work on the historical repetition of identities and their struggle to become fully articulate, something mirrored in other canonical forms (i.e., ideological, national, ethnicracial, etc.), though these are not directly asserted by him.

The structure of the "as if" in relation to one's (always personal) experience, central as it was to the Kantian project, opportunely reappears here as essential, or as foundational even, within the context of Derrida's discussion of his relation to Judaism. This fact is not something that can be lightly glossed over; indeed, it figures as *the* determining factor behind his religious formulations on the whole. In what may be the lengthiest, and yet most decisive, sentence of his essay "Abraham, the Other," he ties the conditional "as if" to his own religious (non)identity as the central feature of his work:

I introduce myself both as the least Jewish, the most unworthy Jew [*le Juif le plus indigne*], the last to deserve the title of authentic Jew, and at the same time, because of all this, by reason of a force of rupture that uproots [*déracinante*] and universalizes the place, the local, the familial, the communal, the national, and so on, he who plays at playing [*joue à jouer*] the role of the most Jewish of all, the last and therefore the only survivor fated to assume the legacy of generations, to save the response or responsibility before the assignation, or before the election, always at risk of taking himself for another [*se prendre pour un autre*], something that belongs to the essence of an experience of election; as if the least could do the most, but also as if [*comme si*] (you will have noted, no doubt, that I often have recourse to the "as if," and I do so intentionally, without playing, without being facile, because I believe that a certain *perhaps* of the *as if* [*peut-être du comme si*], the poetical or the literary, in sum, lies at the heart of what I want to entrust to you)—*as if* the one who disavowed the most, and who appeared to betray the dogmas of belonging, be it a belonging to the community, the religion, even to the people, the nation and the state, and so on—*as if* this individual alone represented the last demand [*l'exigence dernière*], the hyperbolic request of the very thing he appears to betray by perjuring himself.[31]

As this passage illuminates quite directly, it is the aporia/antinomy of experience itself—that is, of those laws that structure it, and that Kant had tried to make peace with by first suggesting the absolutely essential nature of the "as if"—that Derrida finds emblematically demonstrated within the historical "heritage" of religious experience, even, and especially, his own religious experience as a J/jew.[32] Yet, it seemingly is also an "as if" that goes beyond the religious representations that litter our world. There is a core beyond it that nonetheless comes from within it, a "*perhaps* of the *as if*" that opens him up to "the poetical or the literary, in sum, [what] lies at the heart of what I want to entrust to you." In many ways, this religious reconsideration in his work—or what I am here approaching as a sort of "spirituality of representation" itself—is merely an outgrowth of his earlier critique of the metaphysics of presence that he discerned to be at work in Husserl's phenomenology, bringing into sharp relief any attempt to present the phenomena itself, *as such*, and any poetic/religious attempt to do likewise. Derrida repeatedly tries to place himself midway between a phenomenological approach and a Kantian regulative principle, as a ceaseless oscillation between the two wherein one's heritage(s), even of the religious kind, appear as relevant to staking one's identity.

His own Judaic roots, of course, were not something he hid from public view; indeed, he confesses a certain pride in his "jewishness." Yet, there was also a proximate distance which he took with regard to its practices and with the manner in which it makes its mark upon those who profess it as a "living faith" in some sense. Hence, he is able to suggest that it is a "law [*loi*] that comes upon me, a law that, appearing antinomian, dictated to me, in a precocious and obscure fashion, in a kind of light whose rays are unbending, the hyper-formalized formula of a destiny devoted to the secret—and that is why I play seriously, more and more, with the figure of the marrano: the less you show yourself as jewish, the more and better jew you will be."[33] Perhaps such sentiments do express a desire to live "as if" he were not "jewish" in order to become *more* "jewish," though, of course, this leaves wide open the question of whether there could even be a J/jew in the first place, of whether a "jew" could be said to exist at all. And this comment might serve to explain why he considered himself to be "the last to deserve the title of authentic Jew."

For Derrida, it would seem, simply respecting the demands of the other before us (their "hyperbolic, excessive" demand), and therefore truly being hospitable to all others, is only possible through this renunciation of a "certain dogmatism of the place or of the bond (communal, national, religious, of the state)."[34] Only in this way are we opened up toward a responsibility "without limits," a state that is itself illuminated against the messianic horizon of justice. This would be an eschatology forever severed from any teleology.[35] In this sense, living "as if" he were not "jewish" would certainly seem to be the most faithful approximation to the Abrahamic core of Judaism. It would also bear a certain affinity with those readings of Paul and the nature of the "as not" that seemed to condition his decision to live as a Jew to the Jew and as a Gentile to the Gentile, *as if* he were both, or neither—a point that is more fully on display in the work of Giorgio Agamben.[36]

I would suggest at this juncture that the conditional nature of the "as if" finds firmer roots in Derrida's work than it did within the Kantian system, it would seem, firmer because more open to its own conditionality, less likely to fall victim to an ontotheological "metaphysics of presence" which would otherwise seek to conceal its own violence, or wrongly attempt to posit something like the existence of God, a proposition that Derrida would never have sought to defend or even elucidate as such. This would apparently be something of the Heideggerian influence within Derrida's work, a movement away from the ontotheological heritage of providing justifications for God's existence in order to "seal the gaps" within the cracks of all representations. Such a position is what at one point caused him, no doubt, to look for the *renvois* (or traces) between representation and presentation that refused to be gathered (or unified) under either heading. Unity was traditionally a religious task, and it has been religion that has most effectively dealt with the complex processes of providing intelligible representations by which humanity can continue to identify itself in relation to its animality, sexuality, race, and divinity.[37] But this unity, of course, cannot be maintained in the face of the structural reality of *différance*, which also refuses to be present.[38] Such a quest to maintain unity would be nothing more than ideology pure and simple.

Historically speaking, however, religious tradition is nearly all we have before us, and is, therefore, what should most concretely concern Derrida if the claims of representation are to be taken seriously and are not subsequently dismissed. Religious tradition *is* how history has, at times, chosen to record our ongoing struggles with representation. It is only within such "heritages," as he will call them, that representation can be seen to work (and "un-work") itself—that is, where *différance* can be said to function. It is, again, as if between the Jew and the Greek all of history is negotiated. In the context of his struggles with the conditional and its relation to religious belief, the "as if" continues to find its stride as "the oscillation and the undecidability [*l'indécidabilité*] continue, and I would dare say, *must* continue to mark the obscure and uncertain experience of heritage. In any case, I have been unable to put a stop to this experience in me, and it has conditioned the decisions and the responsibilities that have imprinted themselves upon my life."[39] Hence, we discover anew the contradictory positions that his work seemingly had to endorse: "the condition that one emancipate oneself [*s'affranchir*] from every dogma of revelation and election" or see this emancipation as "the very content of the revelation or of the election, their very idea," a ceaseless alternation between presentation and representation that cannot ever be unified or resolved.[40] Indeed, the continuance of an uncertain experience of heritage has given rise to the "formalization," or "most irreducible logic," of the discourses that run throughout his work, from a "messianicity without messianism" to the subject of writing and the trace, from the focus on a democracy always yet "to come" (in contrast to the ontotheological logic of sovereignty) to the subject of *khōra*, or that which grounds any "event of anthropo-theological revelation."[41]

What is really being posited, according to the logic of the "as if" at work in Derrida's thought, is a tendency toward forming a core universal principle uncovered as already operative *within* the Judaic religious heritage, one that signals something of the deconstructive method at work therein. The realization of this tension would insist upon not only the always (un)necessary polarization of our world into Jew and Greek, but also a messianicity over and against an historical messianism, thus also a "jewishness" over against a "judaism." It is, in so many words, the recognition of the other outside us *as* the other *already within* us. Hence, he can word the aporia of how identity is represented as such:

> Either these minimal features are universal and there is no reason to make them into what is proper to the Jew, save to speculate again on the worrying logic of exemplarity; or, as universal as they are, they will have been announced in a unique and precisely exemplary fashion, by election, in a historical revelation; they would then have to do with writing, with memory or with hope in what one calls judaism.[42]

At any rate, a sense of "jewishness" is inseparable from a sense of "judaism," he will tell us, because the former can always root itself in the latter:

> The memory or hope that would constitute jewishness seems to be able to emancipate itself, indeed, from tradition, from the promise and the election proper to judaism. Yet, whether or not one would have to do so, it will always be possible to re-root [*réenraciner*] the very idea and movement of this emancipation, the desire for this emancipation, in a given of judaism, in the memory of an event that, continuing, as it is, to be threatened by amnesia, would remain a history of the gift of the law and would represent the ultimate guardian of the reference to the jewish phenomenon [*la chose juive*].[43]

Judaism remains as a "guardian of jewishness," an aid to its survival, but not necessarily (historically, concretely) as a necessary tradition. There is, perhaps, another way to view the essence of "jewishness" which is, apparently, not entirely indebted to its Judaic roots. This would be, in no uncertain terms, to view "jewishness" as it is in itself, as a spectral force that moves beyond any particular religious tradition, and therefore without its historical Judaic embodiment—which would be an attempt to reconsider Judaic exemplarity through Derrida's reframing of the universal/particular divide along the lines of a spectral messianicity.[44] The shift he is making, and it is a most significant one at that, is one that repeats the movement from transcendental idealism's regulative "as if" to the phenomenological "as such" without actually settling permanently on either one or the other, resting instead rather precariously between both. To see something *as such* is actually to forfeit the desire to ever behold the concrete object itself, exposed *as such* (in an idealist sense), and to rest instead purely in the spectral presence of a failed representation.

In a 1995 interview, Derrida commented on the imagined notion of acting "as if you were dead," an act, he says, that allows us to see objects as they truly are without us, *as such*.[45] And perhaps, this holds the key to understanding not only the manner by which to perceive things as they are, but also how we might allow things to evolve over time into other forms seemingly devoid of their historical rooting—that is, to achieve an approximation of universality without its empirical, historical grounding. There is an "as suchness" beyond the traditional representations of things, an "as suchness" that allows things to exceed their representations otherwise bound to the structures of the "as if," though it is only accessible through another "as if"—the suspension (bracketing) of the subject, "as if" it were dead. It is only through the apparent failure or "death" of the subject that we can access the very thing we are looking for, and even then in a way wholly unlike what we thought we envisioned. Despite the difficulty of achieving this perspective, however, this viewpoint brings with it the possibility of change and justice within the horizon of a future always yet to come.[46] Ethics begins at this point and in profoundly significant ways.

There is an Abrahamic core to the three monotheisms of the West, according to Derrida, which "affects this tradition in an unpredictable way."[47] Christianity may be, in his opinion, the most "plastic, the most open" religion, but it does not have a monopoly on (or "greater affinity with") the deconstructive project. In effect, it would seem that Derrida's faith ultimately holds a belief in a movement beyond all historical religious projects. What he seems to be suggesting is the embracing of an emancipation *from* religious traditions, one that places more stock in a (Kantian-inspired) conditional, nucleus of potentiality within human experience than in the heritage bequeathed to him and to so many others—though such a belief does not rule out a "return to religion" altogether in the end. The element to be universalized within religious experience is what I would call the poetic core of faith (the "as such"), a core that exceeds every historical representation (the "as if") and yet is inseparable from them, because to be glimpsed *as such* requires that one be bracketed *as if* they were dead. In the failure of the subject—its death—we encounter for the first time the object we have been searching for, and it is precisely *this* possibility that brings to light the unique (poetic) potentiality of the human being.

In many ways, Derrida seems to suggest that to behold God is to live *as if* there were none; to witness the spirit, one must look to the failure of the subject—a point I will return to in the following chapters. What we should keep in mind is that only in this way, Derrida suggests, can the poetical and literary inheritance he intends for us be received. This is a point I will take much to heart as I seek to unveil more of this inheritance in the thinkers and poets whose works I will take up in a moment.

Mourning for the Other That I Am

Derrida's occasional reflections upon the processes of mourning seem to resonate deeply with his remarks on religion. Just as one cannot fully incorporate the lost object being mourned—always, rather, being suspended between a more or less successful and a more or less failed incorporation of the beloved—so too does Derrida's Judaism seem to be a failed representation that yet breathes life into a tired and somewhat stale depiction of what it means to be a Jew—a maneuver not wholly unfamiliar to Christians immersed within the legacy of Pauline thought that stands behind them.[48] It becomes, in this precise sense, that which he cannot fully appropriate, or take up in name if he is to be responsible to it, and yet that which must be taken up nonetheless.[49] It is as if Derrida had penned another book, one through which he was able to mourn the death of his many "Judeities," much as he was able to mourn the loss of so many others throughout his lifetime—but a "Judeity" that, nonetheless, permeated his being Jewish and which he had no desire to deny or renounce.[50]

As almost a direct counterfoil to the many deaths that Derrida often found himself mourning, another theme creeps up in his work, one immersed in life and that seemingly propels humanity forward into its own present. Poetry, for him, captures something of the "life of language" that is intertwined with the "work of mourning" that Derrida sees as central to formulating a "hauntology" as it were.[51] If the "endless desertification of language," which signals a "rage against language," is what Derrida associates with the impossibility of saying God's name, as he suggests elsewhere, then it is poetry that seems to reaffirm the existence of the self against this profane horizon.[52] This affinity, which runs throughout the entire poetic enterprise, can be glimpsed in the context of his discussion of the poetry of Paul Celan, where Derrida takes the occasion to reflect upon the manner in which poetry itself attempts to confirm the present moment, to provide a sense of contemporaneousness that comes to rearticulate the precarious and strange placement of the human being at the boundary between human and animal, and which I will address more directly in a moment.[53] It is a present/presence that poetry discloses that is the impossible "I," a gesture that says "this is my body," or "in memory of me," within each poem.[54] Poetry enables us to step outside of our human selves, to see the strange within us and to articulate, in words or through the act of writing, the conditional nature of the beings that we are, to present the "as suchness" of life, or things merely as they are.[55] This is the poetic heritage that Derrida seizes upon as the fundamental gesture of constructing the human being through its expression of our experience, and it seems directly to have picked up where religion, with its representations indebted to the "as if," left off.

Derrida's fidelity is not necessarily to his Judaic roots per se, but to the "jewishness" that pervades every act of reciting the "mourner's Kaddish," or the gesture which confronts the impossibility of authentically incorporating the losses we have suffered in this life. This "jewishness" is the "as suchness" of the believer beyond the "as if-ness" of "judaism." The fragile sense of self, the "I" formed in such a way as to be apart from and yet indebted to the conditional representations before us, is what is created in the poetic gesture to affirm the existence of the self despite the apparent falsity of its representations. It is an act that stands along with ancient Cadmus and proclaims fidelity to that which cannot be proven to exist—though rather than this being about God, it is about the self, and how it can be embraced, though not certainly defined, an act of representation (or its iterability) as it were. Though the human being may not be able to fully, finally, articulate his or her place within the animal kingdom, or in relation to the divine, it can at least strive to find itself within its own present—*as such*—as a being with experiences that can be expressed and represented to itself, for itself, always striving to be more just in their approximation of what it means to be a being *as such*. It is this universal, poetic core of potentiality within our "being human" that Derrida finds circumscribing (or, he might say, "circumcising") the essences of how we identify ourselves (*as such*) over and beyond what has come to identify us (*as if*), and which was, according to him, all he ever really wrote about.[56]

(Perhaps, in the end, this would not place him as far from Kearney's work as Kearney himself seems to indicate at times. Rather, the establishment of a representative narrative for itself would seem to be part of Derrida's project as well, though it is one that is necessarily interrupted by the presence of an other that cannot ever be brought under this narrative structure. This is to say, it is the invention of the other at work in our identities that exceeds the realm of representations that are otherwise *for us* or *for themselves*.[57] It is truly an "invention of the other" that grounds any invention of the self, a religious statement or a declaration of mourning as much as anything else.)

I am given over at the end of these reflections on the nature of the "as if" in Derrida's thought, perhaps appropriately, to Pamela Gillilan's reflections upon the death of her husband given in a collection of poems on the effects of mourning, and which end with a poem that seemingly invokes an imperative that Derrida would seem to have shared in: "Write."[58] As she works it through,

ure as the only subject matter really worth expressing. Moreover, it is not a coincidence that ruins often become sacred spaces over time. "Secular" pilgrimages are often made to such ruinous sites and many speculative hopes and dreams have been placed upon the tiniest archaeological scrap that promises us the hope of building either a museum or shrine—and, in this era, it matters little which one, as they both embody the same atmosphere, generally speaking. With written records, one need only consider the importance placed upon the poetic fragments of Sappho or of the pre-Socratic thinkers, for example, to witness how such "ruins" actually serve to heighten our imagination rather than limit it. We mine such incomplete corpuses for a sense of illumination that offers to go beyond our current patterns of thought—indeed to complete and fulfill what remains lacking in our constructed systems. Therefore, authors as diverse as Ludwig Wittgenstein, Walter Benjamin, Dietrich Bonhoeffer, and Simone Weil continue to appeal to and inspire us, not necessarily because their work is a form of reasoned perfection, but because we continue to find ingenious ways to insert *ourselves* between their fragmented (and often unpublished) thoughts.

Even within the most systematic and prolific of authors there is to be found a fascination with the incomplete or the fragmentary that draws us in for a closer examination. Immanuel Kant's movement from metaphysics to (an incomplete) aesthetics, if seen from this angle, could be said to emphasize the decline of metaphysical (transcendent) structures and a focus upon the entrance of the sublime within the cracks of an ordered reality (rather than the dominance of a transcendent beauty as such). This is a decisive turn revealed in the fracturing of representation that his incomplete critique of judgment sensed, but was not able to fully articulate.[1] Hermeneutics, for its part, in some sense begins with this evolving problematic within the Kantian system—itself an event that took place somewhere between his second and third *Critiques*. It was Kant's attempt to present aesthetics as a suturing of the split between transcendental structures and the experience of the sublime—that is, his trying to bring the sublime experience *into* history—that opened up a space for hermeneutical reasoning to appear. For this reason, and because it can assert itself within this fissure, hermeneutics springs almost fully formed from this disjuncture in Kantian thought. In a direct sense, our contemporary worship of fragments and ruins seems to bear witness to our subsequent inability to let go of such "failed" efforts to wed the transcendent with the historical, a problem no less problematic for Derrida than it was for Kant.

Such hermeneutical reasoning is what has lain at the base of our positing of personal subjectivity, but also what tries to speak to those failures bound to be experienced when we confront the limitations of our variously constructed subjective representations.[2] Yet we are also concerned in this with more than just these hermeneutical gestures of trying to make sense of the fragments that appear in these fissures: it is the realm of the existence of language itself, of meaning and metaphor, and hence of the narrative flow of identity, as Paul Ricoeur's work, for one, has carefully demonstrated.[3] Here is found the meaning present within narrative and here as well is where the construction of history itself takes place.

In this light, poetry could be seen as a privileged linguistic form, one that plays with the abyss from which meaning rises. Poetry, through its very nature, plays upon our fragmentary linguistic existence through its invocation and use of enjambment, for example—the unnatural breaks within the fabric of our linguistic building blocks that invoke the brokenness of the fragmentary form, even as they utilize it.[4] Rather than shun the fragmentary or seek to veil it, however, poetry celebrates its existence and points toward such moments of disjuncture—or being "out of joint"—as the site where language's meaning is disclosed, making poetic representation a privileged site of existential-linguistic discovery and insight.

(What I would like to focus on in this chapter is the manner in which poetry could be said to present (or represent) the *failures* or *ruins* of representation (of ourselves, of history, etc.). In other words, we need to take a close look at our failure to represent the sublime object that poetry, for example, seeks to present in some sense, and which is inextricably tied up with the manner in which we continuously seek to constitute ourselves. Such an exploration is forever bound up with our search for meaning in this world, and our search for the divine in a "world" beyond this one as well. Specifically, I want to look at the representations of failure, and hence also the *failures of representation*, as they are discussed through specific philosophical interpretations of the work of the twentieth-century German-Jewish poet Paul Celan, someone for whom the presentation of the sublime through the failures of language—as *the* central task of poetry—remained a privileged chance through which to encounter the other, even, perhaps, the divine. Though I intend to analyze Celan's work through two later interpreters of it—Philippe Lacoue-Labarthe and Jacques Derrida—it is his lasting poetic legacy that motivates the scope and depth of the themes here under discussion. As will soon become clearer, any effort to situate Celan within the history of poetic expressions is an effort to speak as much *beyond* (poetic) representation as it is *within* (poetic) representation, an opportunity for the sublime (perhaps as a form of "divinity") to appear, and that which merges profoundly in Celan's writing with certain strands of the Judaic tradition and the religious aspirations it places before the individual—a point that throws us back to the suggestion uncovered in the first chapter.)

To understand this conjunction of various influences in his poetry, we might first notice the haunting hollowness within the poetry of Paul Celan, one often mirrored, it might be suggested, in the barren landscapes of Anselm Kiefer's artwork.[5] What such artistic representations try to point to is the failure of representation itself, the crack or gap in the semantic meaning before us that can often direct us toward new cultural constructions or possibilities beyond those we have come to know. Along those lines, I think of Celan's poem "Nocturnally Pouting," with its emphasis upon the death of the word that is yet directed by our hands "towards heaven."

Nächtlich geschürzt
die Lippen der Blumen,
gekreuzt und verschränkt
die Schäfte der Fichten,
ergraut das Moos, erschüttert der Stein,
erwacht zum unendlichen Fluge
die Dohlen über dem Gletscher:

dies ist die Gegend, wo
rasten, die wir ereilt:

sie warden die Stunde nicht nennen,
die Flocken nicht zählen,
den Wassern nicht folgen ans Wehr.

Sie stehen getrennt in der Welt,
ein jeglicher bei seiner Nacht,
ein jeglicher bei seinem Tode,
unwirsch, barhaupt, bereift
von Nahem und Fernem.

Sie tragen die Schuld ab, die ihren Ursprung beseelte,
sie tragen sie ab an ein Wort,
das zu Unrecht besteht, wie der Sommer.

Ein Wort—du weisst:
eine Leiche.

Lass uns sie waschen,
lass uns sie kämmen,
lass uns ihr Aug
himmelwärts wenden.

[Nocturnally pouting
the lips of flowers,

criss-crossed and linked
the shafts of the spruces,
turned grey the moss, the stone shaken,
roused for unending flight
the jackdaws over the glacier:

this is the region where
those we've caught up with rest:

they will not name the hour,
they will not count the flakes
nor follow the stream to the weir.

They stand apart in the world,
each one close up to his night,
each one close up to his death,
surly, bare-headed, hoar-frosted
with all that is near, all that's far.

They discharge the guilt that adhered to their origin,
they discharge it upon a word
that wrongly subsists, like summer.

A word—you know:
a corpse.

Let us wash it,
let us comb it,
let us turn its eye
towards heaven.[6]]

Such a turning of the eye of the corpse of the word may be a protest, or a form of witness; it may be a yearning for the divine, or it may be a defiant recognition of one's abandonment. It is, at least, a record of where things stand, as well as a mirror facing reality that has also been shattered. To see the world as this poem imagines it is to see things *as if* one were already dead, caught up in the gaze of a corpse's eye, and only *as such* able to look toward a future horizon that provides an eschatological hope in a word that not only does not look toward its origins—something Derrida would himself be highly critical of—but also sustains itself, almost miraculously, longer than it should, "wrongly" subsisting "like summer."

Despite Celan's testimony to the ruins of culture, language and religion, there are those who would yet consider his writing as deftly attempting to mobilize the medium of poetry in order to interject a presence *beyond* representation into our world. Following upon what I have already analyzed in chapter 1, but expanding here in the direction of the poetics of representation, Derrida's own subtle reading of Celan's poetry could, in fact, be registered as a comment upon the medium of poetry itself as something of a sovereign endeavor, or an endeavor of sovereignty—that is, an attempt to *establish a (sovereign) self* through its promise to present the "thing itself" (*as such*), that which Derrida deems an absolute impossibility, as we have already seen. However, we might yet ask, is there another way to utilize the link between presence and aesthetics, perhaps such as found in the analysis of Philippe Lacoue-Labarthe and his portrayal of Celan's poetry as an *experience* of subjectivity—as well as of prayer, for example—in order to provide a fitting response to Derrida's interpretation?

Tracing this line of study into Celan's poetry from Derrida to Lacoue-Labarthe reveals a further deepening of our inquiry that must equally be pursued and that too springs from the fissures in a sort of Kantian reasoning. For example, what exactly do the aesthetics of poetry offer us in terms of (transcendental) subject formation? Is there an offer of transcendence that the poem presents us with, and, if so, what is the relationship between such an offering and the modern quest to instantiate a transcendental subjectivity? And so at last, and in order to view the significance of the fragment alongside the construction of our poetic selves, we must ask: were such gestures directly present in Celan's poetry, in his portrayal of the very disintegration of the traditional poetic subject? Is there a creative, poetic force within the failures of language, and, if so, what can such an experience provide for us in terms of hope and spirituality today?

Reflecting the Kantian transition from metaphysics to aesthetics, such questions can be potentially illuminated through the juxtaposition of these varied readings of Celan's work in order to elucidate, not only the decline of metaphysics (and religion alongside it) in the modern era which took place amidst an elevation of aesthetics, but also the presentation of an aesthetics of possibility precisely *as* the *potentiality of aesthetics,* and so of the subject as well. As I will argue in this exposition of the problematic, such a shift in thinking is an attempt to view aesthetics as deeply and continuously immersed in both an encounter with the other and also with the potentiality of our being, a dynamic tension that poetry uniquely addresses. Such an understanding of our potential for developing artistic expressions in the face of the failures of representation that define our symbolic-linguistic existence, I will suggest, opens wide the floodgates for forming creative subjectivities, ones aware of the failures of representation, but nonetheless, predisposed toward presenting failure itself as the only possible means for recognizing the precariousness of human existence. In this last sense, aesthetics takes on an ethical dimension that should neither be overlooked nor underplayed. It also, I will conclude, opens us up to those poetic and creative forces within us that help us to portray our relationships to various representations as a spirituality of sorts, one ever in need of greater theological elucidation.

Derrida on Celan and Poetic Representation

Though remarks on a possible poetic gesture beyond representation or signification may seem to be well removed from general thoughts upon the mystical, I would wager that certain poetic endeavors lie at the center of what we have often considered the mystical (or a negative theology) to be. It is an encounter with a presentation beyond our rationalized representations, something at the heart of most philosophical reflection over the last century or so as well—and that which often invokes labeling such studies as a "return to the religious."[7] We can see this as a connection that certainly lies at the heart of the work of Derrida—even if there is a certain distance he takes from any possible presentation *as such*—for whom the act of representation put forth through language, through the *text* which is all we have, is indispensable to our identities as subjects.[8] For Derrida, there is only the "as if" of representations, the strong metaphors of language upon which our constructions of self are dependent, as I argued in chapter 1.[9] We are inseparably connected to this reality, according to Derrida, no matter how greatly we might wish to be separated from it. Indeed, in some sense, any attempt to be sovereign (politically) seems to stem, for him, from the attempt to remove oneself from the linguistic bonds that hold us all in check. Hence, it is within the context of his remarks on sovereign power that he situates his reading of Celan's poetry.[10]

It might also be helpful to keep in mind at this point that Derrida famously said that his work was not a negative theology.[11] Negative theology so often leads to a presence, he felt; indeed, it invokes a (transcendent) presence through its very prayers and, in this sense, is to be considered as a form of mystical thinking, of mystical theology as well as a sovereign theology or a theology *of* sovereignty. (And it is perhaps not surprising, within this line of thought, that a mystical thinker like Pseudo-Dionysius was one of the first to designate a hierarchical order existing in heaven that was incorporated directly into his vision of ecclesiology.)

What Derrida is seeking to get at, for his part, is the structure behind (and *beyond*) theology, the existence of language as it has shaped and conditioned our every constructed theology: "Language has begun without us, in us, before us [*Le langage a commence sans nous, en nous avant nous*]. This is what theology calls God, and it is necessary, it will have been necessary to speak [*il aura fallu parler*]."[12] Yet this, for him, is not something we can present in any sense. It is the "text" that is given, a representation that is attached to us and that is all that there is to work with. Moreover, as he makes clear elsewhere, consciousness itself is inseparable from language and from representation, that is, from the establishment of the human subject over and against its animality.[13] The anthropologies that sustain these borders (and our Judeo-Christian theological ones as well) are themselves dependent upon the aporetic nature of our existence, the impossibility of accurately describing what we are *as such*, in itself, or rather in ourselves.[14]

This is the first critique of the *as such*-ness that Derrida will mount, and this is the same critical logic that will frame his many debates with those genealogists whose methods he finds objectionable: Sigmund Freud, Michel Foucault, Giorgio Agamben—figures all lost in the archives, according to him, searching for the presentation of the "thing itself."[15] There may be something there, out beyond us, a true *presence* lingering before us, but it is something we can neither find a way to represent nor to experience as a pure presentation. For Derrida, being responsible for the unrepresentable thing, the "wholly other" who is always the other before us, means enduring the experience and condition (and, hence, limitation) of our aporetic existence, realizing only then that we are dependent upon language and inescapably bound to it, that the thing itself cannot be presented without mediation and must be respected as ultimately unknowable. In this state, we can locate his many discussions of the aporia of the *possible* impossible, as well as the *impossible* possible, and the experience of possibility *as* impossibility. The attempt to experience this limit directly and without mediation marks, for Derrida, the prominent rise of the "as such," what everything can be said to wait for (its form of messianicity), and as its potential appearance effaces the borders and boundaries upon which all of our representations rely.[16]

The crossing of borders and boundaries, of course, is what defines an apophatic theology tout court, precisely what Derrida does *not* wish to engage in because he believes it *cannot* be engaged with *as such*.[17] We must endure the aporia, Derrida cautions, which, strictly speaking, cannot be *endured as such*: "the ultimate aporia is the impossibility of the aporia *as such*."[18] There is no more originary path to take than this experience of the inexperienceable that must be endured, but not contorted into some form of presence. The event *as such* does not itself appear because it is *too* monstrous; if it did appear, we would not be able to reason, or to think the future.[19] Negative theology, for its part, attempts to surpass the aporia which cannot be exceeded within reason, and Derrida, who is far too Kantian in this respect, cannot acknowledge any such possibility.[20] This same relationship between the "as if" and the "as such" that Derrida plays upon can be seen more clearly in his writings on the poetry of Celan, a more than occasional subject of study for him, and for good reason, as I intend to show.[21]

In the context of a series of lectures devoted to exploring the concept of sovereignty, Derrida contends that poetry portrays a certain (sovereign) sense of majesty through its language, yet it does not present what it attempts to present; it only bears witness to a presence that cannot be presented—a point that shares a good deal in Agamben's analysis of the glory that covers the empty throne of sovereign power.[22] As he puts it, "Majesty is here majestic, and it is poetry, insofar as it bears witness [*témoigne*] to the present, the now, the 'presence' . . . of the human."[23] Derrida himself, of course, would not favor a primacy of presence that Celan, perhaps, had sought to establish within the majesty of the poem. He says as much immediately following his acknowledgment of how important this primacy to presence was for Celan. Such a statement is also in keeping with the Derrida who had launched numerous attacks on the "metaphysics of presence," which attempts to posit itself as sovereign within the history of Western thought.[24]

As he often put it, the poem, or poetics in fact, has a secret, in essence that it "conceals itself by exhibiting its concealment *as such*."[25] It is a concealment that can be "shown" as *only* being a concealment—it does not show the content of the secret itself. And secrets, we are told elsewhere, are always involved in acts of representation, though they themselves cannot be represented.[26] Derrida will even venture so far on this point to assert that the poetic work "perhaps no longer derives from self-presentation *as such*," only from the exposure of what it is intent to conceal.[27] Hence, we are left to speculate as to how much presence, sacrality, revelation, or religious desiring *could* even be present in our world, since all that these terms could potentially testify to would be the absence of any genuine presence. How much of it indeed could *be* present since our (theo)poetics is no longer able to arise from a presumed presentation of the thing itself?[28]

What he seems to be wholeheartedly deconstructing is a possible poetic presence beyond the political present, a majesty of the event beyond the majesty of political power, and this as a distinction with wider implications that Derrida only hints toward at times, or circles around, as if indicating that there could be something more there to be taken up, but which presently is not. If it were to be taken up, this would be something that opens up Derrida's own writing toward a specific poetic lineage that ranges from Wallace Stevens to Adrienne Rich, and perhaps even to the critical analyses of Lacoue-Labarthe and Agamben—both of whom I will be dealing with in a moment—yet which also keeps him at a certain distance from them all, refusing to concede that there is anything beyond our representations that we can access *as such*.[29] His not taking up this line of poetic tradition, to my mind, is a great missed opportunity and one that I am directly looking to move closer toward in what follows, because I believe it can offer us another way to view this apparent impasse.

Despite such a missed opportunity, Derrida does discover an approach to the event contained within Celan's poetry that is not an essence or an origin locatable within the poetic experience—and this in itself is a very valuable insight worth reflecting on a great deal.[30] There is consequently for him a majesty of the present within the poetic that *is* sovereign, and that calls us to it, though it is not a politically sovereign form as would befit a king, for example. It is a stepping outside of the human being that is, he says, proper to artistic representations, proper perhaps even for theological speculations, but not for a strictly speaking philosophical methodology.[31] It is no less than a division of those already existing political divisions, a double division, or a division of division itself, that poetry undertakes as an *other* form of majesty yet wholly foreign to philosophy—but which is more rather than less effective within our world: it challenges and rearticulates our political and religious spheres despite the inaccessibility it presents to philosophy.[32]

Such a theopoetics is not the proper subject of philosophical inquiry, to be sure, though this does not stop Derrida from trying to access the source of its (sovereign) power or majesty. This tension certainly calls to mind at least the manner in which the philosophical needs the nonphilosophical, or in which thinking needs the unthought in order to maintain its own inner integrity, as figures as diverse as Theodor Adorno and Gilles Deleuze had themselves suggested. Speaking of the two foreigners present in the poem, for example—a difference somewhat like the "passage of poetry" that Celan identifies as possible in order for humanity to see beyond itself—Derrida draws upon the difference between them in order to attempt to locate something of the present event within the poetic. As he puts it:

> This is the difference, in the punctuality of the now [*la ponctualité du maintenant*], in the pinpoint of the present moment, of *my* present, between *on the one hand*, my other living present (retained or anticipated by an indispensable movement of retention and pretension), and, *on the other hand*, wholly other, the present of the other the temporality of which cannot be reduced, included, assimilated, introjected, appropriated into mine, cannot even resemble it or be similar to it, a present or proper time of the other that I must surely let go, radically giving it up, but also the very possibility of which (the *perhaps* [*peut-être*] beyond all knowledge) is the chance both of

the encounter [*la rencontre*] (*Begegnung*) and of this event, this advent [*cette venue*], of what is called poetry. An improbable poetry ("who knows") but a poetry to take one's breath away and turn it [*à couper et à tourner le souffle*], and so also turn life and path, which can still be a path of art both wider and narrower.[33]

Playing upon Celan's use of the compound word *"Atemwende"* or "breath-turn," Derrida elaborates upon an "improbable poetry" that contains the ability to "take one's breath away and turn it," and that appears to have a real bearing upon how we define, or *cease to define* ourselves within this space.[34] This is done, according to him, without an actual presence of the other being presented. It is rather, structurally speaking, a part of our struggle with the "wholly other" before us, an openness that must be maintained, seemingly, to openness itself. It is a summons to keep us "present" to ourselves, to that which is always beyond us, always singular, always an event at the heart of those aporias that constantly define and yet elude us. It is the nonphilosophical within the philosophical, if you will, that somehow yet sustains philosophy and is, therefore, albeit indirectly at times, its subject.

In so many words, I am suggesting that this is what he will speak of elsewhere as an *envoi*, or "sending," that is foreign to representation and yet is not exactly gathered under the label of presence either. It is a "pre-ontological" (or "pre-ontotheological") sending that does not gather itself at all under any singular heading; it is, rather, gathered only through its dividing of itself, an act that occurs within itself and not in the presentation of an other (as a presence) from without. As he puts it in this context, there is nothing present before it as it is only "the other in itself without itself," an act of carrying the other before us without affixing identity to either them or us.[35] Perhaps then, if we can dare to state it, there is a *presentation beyond representation*—or perhaps better, a space beyond both and *in* the failures of each—that lurks unstated underneath his work on language, undergirding its strength and not so far off, in the end, from other attempts to locate a presence seemingly beyond us. As Derrida indicates within his earlier remarks on Celan, there is, ultimately, a *poetic* revolution possible within the *political* revolution, a revolution within the living present that is also a "dethroning of majesty [*dethronement de la majesté*]" which goes beyond all forms of knowledge and yet undergirds all claims to know.[36] As we had previously been told by Derrida, there is a faith in poetry that is a faith in God [*"Foi en la poésie comme foi en Dieu, ici en la majesté du présent"*], a present faith *itself present* within the majesty of the poem.[37] Lurking in such a pronouncement is perhaps a new vision of faith, of poetry, and of those subjectivities formed through such an experience. And yet it is a vision that Derrida indicates only *might* be possible.

Lacoue-Labarthe on Celan

With Celan's poetry, a certain difficulty confronts us when we are concerned with its interpretation, as he has often been accused of being hermetic or at least tremendously obscure. For Philippe Lacoue-Labarthe, Celan's poetry, however, goes beyond such charges as it escapes interpretation altogether—in fact, his poetry *prohibits* it.[38] This is the case, for Lacoue-Labarthe, because his poetry seeks to go back to its own origins and yet to challenge the very experience of the singular, of singularity itself.[39] The poem, we are told, is absolutely singular, and it calls its reader into a singular paradigm that *cannot be co-opted into a larger (hermeneutical) field of operations*.[40] Hence we are to be solely concerned with the limits of aesthetics and the rise of singular forms. This was Celan's unique *gesture*, according to Lacoue-Labarthe, as his poetry sought to exceed the bounds of language, an experience for him of living life after the destruction and desolation of the Jewish people at the hands of their German masters.[41] There was then, as Derrida put it, a possible faith lurking in Celan's poetry, one open to that which seemingly lies beyond the poem itself.

The real question for Celan in the age of the decline of the subject is what it means to go out of one's self (*sortir de soi*) as one goes beyond the poem, and to encounter the fragility of dialogue without a traditional (hermeneutical) anchor mooring us to the ground.[42] To experience a poem in its singularity is an experience of estrangement or even of "forgetting oneself [*l'oubli de soi*]" as Lacoue-Labarthe will later center his remarks.[43] I would only add to this that such an estrangement from oneself—the very essence of *exilic* living, you might say—may provide us with another vantage point from which to read the nature of the sublime experience, or Derrida's efforts to locate a space not quite at home with either presentation or representation. It is ultimately through poetry that "estrangement yields ground to the encounter [*L'étrangement cede le pas à la rencontre*]," as Lacoue-Labarthe puts it.[44] What the American poet Adrienne Rich, for example, has described as a presentation of the thing itself (here borrowing a conceptual imagery from her predecessor Wallace Stevens), and as I will take up soon in what follows, seems almost possible within poetry as an encounter within the singular experience of the poem itself. It occurs in the coupling of voices that merge within its hearing and which yet wholly transcends the singular context of any particular poem (in its unique particularity) or any person (in their absolutely unique particularity) for that matter. Rich's poetry, for its part, is also exilic, though it is one that speaks to our ability to *couple* with other voices, other persons, other poets, and not necessarily one that sought an encounter as fixedly as Celan's poetry because it sang also of encounters, not just those longed for, but those *already experienced.*

Despite this possible critique of Celan's poetry, which yearned for an encounter that one suspects he may never have felt as adequately as he desired, there is something essential to his longing that informs our understanding of the nature of poetry itself that cannot be overlooked. Again, this longing captured in poetic form—by the form of the poem itself even—seems to reveal the fracturing of the Kantian (transcendental) subject in a manner that allows the fragments to reveal themselves as the very fabric of the human being that cannot simply be sutured into a whole. In terms that foreshadow Paul Ricoeur's emphasis on the nature of canonical forms as one of binding-unbinding (and akin to Derrida's term "stricture"[45]), as well as his defining of the self *as* another,[46] Lacoue-Labarthe presents Celan's original reading of the poetic encounter as that which sustains the very organization of such a process:

> [T]he encounter [*la recontre*] is no less abysmal than estrangement. As soon as the other occurs, as such [*comme tel*], there is the threat of an absolute alterity [*altérité absolue*]: ab-solute, which forbids or renders impossible all relation. The other, if it is indeed other, is immediately the wholly other [*tout autre*]. But at the same time, the other, even if wholly other, is, insofar as it is other, unthinkable without relation to the same [*rapport au même*]: as soon as [the] other appears, detaching itself from the same, the same, in advance, has already recovered it and brought it back. It is impossible to think a total unbinding [*une pure déliaison*].[47]

Not total perhaps, but certainly partial. The poem, in some sense, ushers in a messianic encounter that undoes the self it must now watch re-create itself, or re-form itself entirely, indebted still to the fragmentary form of the poetic for its self-support.

Referring to Derrida's notion of *différance*, Lacoue-Labarthe presents us with an indication of the self that is divested from *within*, forever split *from* itself and seeking to return *to* itself. This is a preparation within the self for an *other* self to appear before it, the encounter within an estrangement that characterizes the human experience of being other to others as well as to oneself.[48] The question before us thereby remains: can Celan's singular poem, the poem of the singular, be brought within such a field of (more or less) hermeneutical operations? That is, can the nature of art be seen as a series of singularities rupturing and breaking with tradition and as yet somehow essential to the processes *of* a given poetic tradition? Celan's art invokes this question, indeed makes this question a necessary inquiry placed before all artistic attempts at expression, suggesting a sort of model of "discontinuity *as* continuity," or the failures of representation as the only true representation, as the only possible way forward for thought.

As Lacoue-Labarthe develops this thought further, the poem begins to break through our constructed realities in order to shatter them and is also at the same time the very fabric of these same realities. The poem becomes the entrance of a "natural" building block of perception itself. As he describes this state of things, "The poem (the poetic act), in this mode proper to it (dialogue), is the thought of the present's presence [*la presence du présent*], or of the other of what is present: the thought of no-thingness [*né-ant*] (of Being), that is to say, the thought of time."[49] This is the natural flow of time, again, interrupting our neatly crafted representations with its presence beyond our ability to comprehend it.[50]

Accordingly, there is no doubt that the experience of reading Celan's poems, for Lacoue-Labarthe, is one of an "interdiction against representation," an opening up to a horizon of the unpresentable or unfigurable.[51] It is in this sense that Lacoue-Labarthe designates Jewish messianism (here aligned with Martin Buber, Gershom Scholem, and Walter Benjamin) as the "response" to the traditional forms of sacred poetry embodied in poets such as Friedrich Hölderin.[52] Here, we encounter the link between such failures of representation and the spiritual forces that somehow link our varied representations together. It is a form of sacrality, or, rather, a spirituality, that is entirely ordinary, common, and profane. It is the *least* sacred thing which somehow manages, because of its absolute "profanity," to provide the only real vestige of sacrality possible. It is a new form of attentiveness to the present that will become, in turn, a new form of prayer within the modern world.

The unpresentable comes to us here in the form of a gesture, a "counter-word [contre-*parole*]," one that signifies a reality yet without signification taking place, and is caught in the suspension between these two contradictory positions—perhaps because it is the person that is comprised of a natural interruptive force of "no-thingness," or time itself alone. In many ways, this idea is somewhat more akin to Derrida's notion of the *renvoi* than either author might have been willing to recognize.[53]

Poetry performs a separation inherent in art itself, consequently placing poetry in a unique position as that form that can best demonstrate the catastrophe of language alongside the catastrophe of the subject, demonstrating the divisions and ruptures of representation both *through* and *with* language.[54] No matter if one views it from the perspective of Derrida or of Lacoue-Labarthe, its operations remain the same. As Lacoue-Labarthe himself puts it, "This is why poetry, if it ever occurs [*si jamais elle advient*], occurs as the brutal revelation of the abyss that contains art (language) and nevertheless constitutes it, as such [*comme tel*], in its strangeness [*étrangeté*]."[55] And it is precisely this strangeness, I would further argue, that prevents us from ever fully labeling the poetic process as a monolithic entity—as therefore *definable* in any sense.

This continuous state of (linguistic) interruption will, in turn, be the very thing that enables poetry, as an openness to the wholly other, to be for Lacoue-Labarthe a form of utopia (*l'u-topie*), a place *without* place where revelation *is* yet perhaps possible ("*au lieu sans lieu de l'avènement*").[56] As an always inherently theopoetics, such an openness "does battle" against all forms of idolatry ("*un combat contre l'idolâtrie*") (those *defined* registers) in an effort to present the "thing itself" before us, even if it cannot, in the end, present that thing itself. Such a characterization, moreover, comes to mark the zero degree of revealability, the possibility of an encounter that can be anticipated, but that cannot be properly presented.[57] In other words, it clears a space for a presence to appear—or, to put things in a Derridean idiom, *the minimum gesture of a religious encounter always yet to come.*[58]

What Lacoue-Labarthe ultimately contends is that Celan's poetry opens up a radically new possibility for *prayer*, one that is guarded against the failures of naming (signifying) God and is simultaneously aware of how the context of any such revelation is constituted on the same grounds as that upon which the human being constructs itself—in the openness where a genuine encounter can occur.[59] In this sense, every poem is rightly understood to be a prayer and the possibility for an authentic encounter, yet also a space we all too often fill with empty or idle words in an effort to construct our world, and to be sovereign over it. Celan's poetry arrives, we are told, as confirmation that those traditional prayers uttered to a God who can be named, to the traditional forms of poetry as we have known them, are as dead as the God whom Nietzsche once pronounced deceased.[60] The "Open" now goes from being a sacred space to being profaned, with Celan's poetry remaining as a most significant testament to this fact.[61] Likewise, these traditional forms are now as dead as are certain ontotheological justifications for God's existence.

Despite this, however, perhaps in this entirely immanent realm, another type of encounter is possible, one that moves beyond the realm of (sovereign) transcendence and toward the sublime encounter with the other, the nature of the other that is the nature of our selves.[62] To glimpse something of this new spirituality, however, we must be open to the failures of our representations—of God, of prayer, of poetry, of language, of philosophy—in short, of all we thought stood underneath our feet and yet, in the end, after its destruction (or "deconstruction"), still remains in the same place. From a methodological perspective, this would describe the difficulty of understanding why deconstruction must still work within a hermeneutical framework—that is, why what we have underneath us, grounding us, will change its name from time to time, but will never be done away with altogether.

Derrida's efforts to find a way beyond the dichotomy of presentation/representation involved a turn to Husserl's notion of "appresentation," in order to establish a conceptualization that is, to be sure, not a full presentation. It is, however, something we might consider as aware of the failures of representation.[63] What this realization seems to offer us is a confirmation of Celan's vision for (poetic) representation—that only in the display of our failures can something of a "successful" encounter come about. Celan's ongoing contribution to poetry is, therefore, a continuous deepening of artistic representation itself, one that has gone *through* the very failures of our representations in order to point the way toward a realm the significance of which we have yet to fully grasp. It is, then, if you will, another way in which we might only now begin to *rethink* the theological "beyond" our critiques of the ontotheological.

The world to which we are opened up by Celan's insight is a world that is no world, and yet it offers us new possibilities for relating to one another and hence for constructing ourselves anew. This is a dilemma captured fittingly in Celan's phrasing: "Die Welt ist fort, ich muß dich tragen [The world is gone, I must carry you]."[64] There is, within such thoughts, a profound insight concerning the modern tendency to romanticize ruins as well. Confronting such ruinous reminders, we, as the human race, are often humbled as we seek a more accurate perspective of our own nature, of our relationship to history and of our comprehension of that which is ultimately much greater than us, and which, at times, must carry us through the world. The truth that is opened up by such a formulation of reality was in fact once summarized quite succinctly by Samuel Beckett: we must learn to "fail better." Then, and only then, might we also learn to represent better—our world, divinity, and humanity.

As I have already indicated in chapter 1, for Kant, the regulative principle of the "as if" was essentially all we have to work with in the world of representations.[65] The presentation of a thing *as such*, that is, without mediation, was something inaccessible, and, therefore, beyond what we are capable of comprehending. Ever since, for most philosophers, who indeed often act as guardians of what is considered both possible and impossible within the realm of experience, this limitation has been enough to constrict our understanding of what is other to us and to our own, varied reconstructions of whatever is *re*-presented before us. This is to say, practically speaking, no *thing* can present itself beyond our representations of it.

Despite this seemingly insurmountable obstacle imposed upon us by the limits of thought, philosophical reasoning has often sought to go beyond this Kantian restriction (or "regulation") in order to experience something of a presence beyond representation. As I have argued throughout this chapter, nowhere has this dramatic search been more present than in the realm of poetry, where language continuously circles around the "thing itself," asking it to come forth and present itself *as such*—and despite its failure to do so. Efforts such as these, in turn, have provided ample, and fruitful, material for philosophical and theological reflection, though both fields are often loathe to take up such objects directly.

In the following section, I briefly want to illustrate the tensions between the regulative "as if" and the almost hyperbolic "as such" which attempts to extend itself beyond what we can and do represent both *in* and *through* language. To do so, I will draw upon the poetic legacies of the "as such" in the poetry of Wallace Stevens and Adrienne Rich, two American poets bent on pushing poetry to its limits in order to interrogate what is possible to (re)present within language. In this fashion, I am hoping to illuminate the provocative contrast between poetic efforts aimed at revealing the "thing itself" *as such* and Derrida's insistence upon the necessity of remaining indebted to the "as if."

The Poetic Presentation as such in the Work of Adrienne Rich

There has always been, within poetry, an effort to capture and portray the "thing itself" *as such*, an object as it is in itself, beyond whatever significations we humans can place upon it through our words. This is a doubly difficult task to perform, of course, as poetry is continuously immersed in a project of exposing the existence of language and our relation to it, the shape and contours of this coexistence as well as its capabilities and shortcomings. In the work of Giorgio Agamben, for example, there recently has arisen an intense desire to present (not *re*-present) "The Thing Itself," something he finds at work in the philosophy of Plato as much as in the varied poetries of Dante, Rainer Maria Rilke, or Giorgio Caproni, to name but a few.[66] If anything, what Agamben draws our attention to, time and again, is the failure of language to adequately *present* anything, and how, therefore, we become witness to a poetic drive to go beyond its inscriptions.[67] This is as much a theological issue, we might add (and as Agamben himself does add) as anything else—and it is a subject I will take up in the context of Agamben's work in chapter 3.

This impulse to discern the "thing itself"—the *as such*-ness of a thing beyond its linguistically codified and intelligible form—is what pushes many modern poets to tangle with the failure of language itself, what Adrienne Rich, for one, has often pursued under many names: the "dream of a common language," the "school among the ruins," and perhaps most poignantly, as an act of "diving into the wreck." It is in her poem "Diving into the Wreck" in particular that we are witness to what is maybe the poetic task *par excellence,* and one that deeply resonates with Celan's poetry as we have already seen it. In that poem she describes the act of diving into the vast ocean in search of a sunken wreck that mirrors our daily lives as we have constructed them, and it is there that she discovers:

> the thing I came for:
> the wreck and not the story of the wreck
> the thing itself and not the myth
> the drowned face always staring
> toward the sun
> the evidence of damage
> worn by salt and sway into this threadbare beauty
> the ribs of the disaster
> curving their assertion
> among the tentative haunters[68]

Echoing themes she will describe elsewhere as the reality of having to deal with a patriarchal language that is yet her own—the "oppressor's language," as Celan would elsewhere also call it—Rich seeks to move beyond language, its story and its dominion, in order to examine what lies before her, without words to conceal or distort it.[69] As she will parallel this movement in another poem entitled "An Atlas of the Difficult World":

> . . . I don't want to know
> wreckage, dreck and waste, but these are the materials
> and so are the slow lift of the moon's belly
> over wreckage, dreck, and waste, wild treefrogs calling in
> another season, light and music still pouring over
> our fissured, cracked terrain.[70]

In this return to the wreck, the ruin, the dreck, and the waste that is our language and that is all we have to communicate with, Rich is seeking something beyond language, a presentation of the beings that we are *as such* and, yet, which seem at times to be so distant from the poetry we record with our words.

It comes as little surprise, then, that Rich spends some time toward the end of the collection of poems *Diving into the Wreck* mediating on the figure of a "savage child," one discovered in the woods after having spent years without language, a possible infanticide gone terribly awry. There, as a sort of response to the wreck of language she dives within, she looks to this solitary, wordless figure still bearing the scars of a knife once placed upon his throat as a sort of obverse mirror to our desires for immersion in both language and culture. She imagines how his "rescuers" in fact, hoping to do the right thing,

> . . . tried to care for you
> tried to teach you to care
> for objects of their caring:
>
> ....
>
> to teach you names
> for things
> you did not need
>
> ....
>
> to teach you language:
> the thread their lives
> were strung on[71]

What these meditations produce for Rich, however, is not necessarily sympathetic to the "rescuers" of this wayward "savage" child. Rather, she is prompted through the contemplation of this figure to push beyond language, *to a place prior to language*, a place that will recall Agamben's own attempts to locate an originary site of our "infancy" beyond our linguistic being. As she continues to pursue this imaginative landscape for refashioning our quest for the "thing itself" beyond language:

> Go back so far there is another language
> go back far enough the language
> is no longer personal
>
> these scars bear witness
> but whether to repair
> or to destruction
> I no longer know[72]

This impulse to go beyond, or *before*, language is not something unique to Rich's work, nor to Agamben's; nor is it unfamiliar to Derrida's critique of such gestures as overt efforts to maintain some form of sovereign power.[73] There are numerous poetic examples that could be invoked as prior attempts to push language to its limits and to work through language to a point *beyond* language. Indeed, the desire itself seems to stem from those same regions which Agamben's work will point to, and it is immanently discernable in the poetry of one of Rich's greatest influences— her "liberator" as she puts it—the American poet Wallace Stevens, whom we encountered at the beginning of this book through his efforts to engage with the long legacy of poetic representations and the nature of the "as if."

In an essay devoted to tracing the influence of Stevens's poetry upon her own work, Rich tells us, "It was he [Stevens] who said to me, *Ourselves in poetry must take their place,* who told me that poetry must change, our ideas of order, of the romantic, of language itself must change."[74] Poetry has a power to break through the divisions of our world (such as that of race, which she specifically addresses in this context), and to offer something beyond these linguistically encoded significations. This is what Stevens himself, on numerous occasions, attempted to point toward, writing poems with such metaphysical tones as "Reality Is an Activity of the Most August Imagination," "The Poem That Took the Place of a Mountain," "The Course of a Particular," "The Role of the Idea in Poetry," "Two Illustrations That the World Is What You Make of It," "Of Mere Being," and, perhaps making the point best, his poem "Not Ideas About the Thing but the Thing Itself":[75]

> At the earliest ending of winter,
> In March, a scrawny cry from outside
> Seeming like a sound in his mind.
>
> He knew that he heard it,
> A bird's cry, at daylight or before,
> In the early March wind.
>
> The sun was rising at six,
> No longer a battered panache above snow . . .
> It would have been outside.
>
> It was not from the vast ventriloquism
> Of sleep's faded papier-mâché . . .
> The sun was coming from outside.
>
> That scrawny cry—it was
> A chorister whose c preceded the choir.
> It was part of the colossal sun,

Surrounded by its choral rings,
Still far away. It was like
A new knowledge of reality.[76]

It is in this poem, for example, that he inches ever closer, though the presentation of a thing *as such*, to what he calls "a new knowledge of reality," one stationed beyond the confines of the regulative logic of representations.[77]

It is a new knowledge of reality that opens up new sources of access to the selves that we are, sources that, almost paradoxically, stem from the things (not reduced to either subjects or objects) before us. We are caught up in the *as such*-ness of things, inescapably bound to them, though not identified *through*, *with* or *in* them. As the philosopher Simon Critchley puts it in a study of Stevens's poetry:

> The poetic act, the act of the mind, illumines the surface of things with imagination's beam. This act is part of the thing and not about it. Through it, we detect what we might call *the movement of the self* in those things: plate, bread, wine, water, rock, tree, moon. In poetry, the making of things are makings of the self. Poets are the chanting-hearted artificers of the world in which they sing and, singing, make.[78]

Perhaps what poetry really does, and what both Rich and Stevens attempt to point us toward through their poetry, is to present something beyond those signified representations with which we are so familiar and which help us to limit and identify our cultural standing, but which also violently reduce the fullness of any singularity before us. The poetic self, rather, is one that is open to the things before it, letting them shape it as much as it shapes them. This is, as Lacoue-Labarthe describes it in the context of Paul Celan's poetry, to point to the relevance of the *gesture*, or that which is somehow able to signify something while also being removed from the realm of signification.[79] It is an attempt to present the "thing itself" without reducing it to a common linguistic-symbolic marker, and it is, therefore, a recognition of the failures of language, but also, nonetheless, a taking up of language to bring us to a new awareness of our relationship to language, and so the poetic, but also the theological, the political, the ethical, the philosophical, etc. Poetry can thus attempt to *say existence itself*, and at the same time, to express something of the "catastrophe of language," something more than familiar to Rich's poetic endeavors to explore "the wreck" of reality alongside the contamination of language.

How, then, are we to define a presence that cannot be present outside of our regulative ideals, but only *present* in the aporetic openings that must be cultivated from within? Is this what the many poetic and mystical traditions have actually sought to present to us over the centuries, a presentation of the aporia itself, a presence not beyond the self but one entirely given within it? For Derrida, this is a messianic event that will not end with some determinate content; it is rather part of the structure of the system of representations itself. This is ultimately what allows Derrida to summon Celan once again in yet another context as bearing witness to the opening of multiple "other" poetics without end that are furthered through the opening of this reality.[80]

In this opening, and somewhat akin to Rilke's poetic conceptualization of the "Open" as poetically formulated in his *Duino Elegies*,[81] we bear witness to the profound mystical configuration of the self, a potential form of mysticism that cannot be easily comprehended or codified, but that works according to a regulative logic of the aporia. This is a radical openness that never dies away or tones itself down, but constantly opens itself up to the event before us, *within* us. In the end, what I hear are the echoes of a presence resonating from within, something just barely out of reach, just barely divine, just barely a glimpse of what truth must continue to unwind down the slow, graceful turnings within the animal who is immersed in language. And so, perhaps Rich puts it best when she, the one who dives into the wreck as into the "thing itself," says:

> If from time to time I envy
> the pure annunciations to the eye
>
> the *visio beatifica*
> if from time to time I long to turn
>
> like the Eleusinian hierophant
> holding up a simple ear of grain
>
> for return to the concrete and everlasting world
> what in fact I keep choosing
>
> are these words, these whispers, conversations
> from which time after time the truth breaks moist and green.[82]

On Language and Its Profanation
*Beyond Representation in the Poetic Theory
of Giorgio Agamben*

Despite all of the gestures made by poets toward a realm beyond representation, for Derrida, poetry was more akin to an attempt to present a presence that actually failed to do just that. That is, poetry speaks on the same
level concerning faith—whatever it may or may not be in the end—that
religion does, and both are beyond the certitude of philosophical reasoning. In addition, we might be justified in asking: Is there another way to
view the "faith" we are asked to produce in both cases that is, moreover,
inherent to our human, linguistic condition (as creaturely, rational beings)?
Can we formulate a new vision of language (as a form of representation)
that moves us toward the poetic in a different sense, that opens us up
further not to any transcendent reality necessarily, but to one more fully
immanent to our existence, helping us to develop a creative, poetic spirituality of sorts that resonates with the failures of representation, and that
does not necessarily deviate from Derrida's and Lacoue-Labarthe's under-
standings but compliments them by deepening their accounts in comparison with one another?

The role of the poetic in Giorgio Agamben's work becomes highly significant at this point and can assist us in understanding his philosophy on
the whole, especially in relation to Derrida and the role of representation
within the poetic. As I will seek to demonstrate in this chapter, Agamben's
development of the poetic in relation to philosophy's object of knowledge,
the a/theological, and a realm of potentiality within the human being provides a fitting progression from Derrida and Lacoue-Labarthe toward

a theory of the spiritual and creative failures of representation that I will take up more directly in the conclusion.

From medieval Italian poetry to contemporary theories of the poetic, Agamben utilizes a vast array of literary figures in order to illustrate the evolutionary development of the "human being" in terms of its self-expressiveness and self-definition. For example, in one of his early writings that sought to determine the very nature of poetry, Agamben develops a genealogy of the *corn*, the poetic term representing the "tip" or "extremity" of the poem that has been historically portrayed at once as a woman's body, a "bodily orifice," and "the point of rupture of the strophe's metrical structure."[1] Its use by the medieval poets he surveys was essential to comprehending their love poems, both their sense and their incorporation of the female body. In Agamben's analysis, the use and success of the corn in the poetry of the period was that it resulted in uncovering something fundamental concerning the nature of poetry itself, and consequently of human experience. As we will see Dante illustrate in a moment, the rise of the corn can also be perceived as an attempt to heal some of the more fundamental disjunctions within the human person.

In this particular study by Agamben, the division of emphasis is one between *intellect* and *speech*, though its later reshaping into one between *philosophy* and *poetry*, or *knowledge* and *experience* (as he will elsewhere define it, and which I will take up later) is not hard to discern. Intellect and speech are portrayed as the two fundamental elements of a division that remains a focal point within Agamben's work and which he discerns as essential to understanding the central motivating factors (the *impetus*) for medieval poetry. In this particular context, he will consider how "Dante defines the poetic event not by a convergence but rather by a divergence between intellect and language. This divergence gives rise to a double 'ineffableness' (*ineffabilitade*), in which the intellect cannot grasp ('end') what language says and in which language does not 'completely follow' what the intellect comprehends."[2] Foreshadowing the impending scission between poetry and philosophy within the modern period, Dante himself seems to have relied quite heavily, though in a nuanced fashion, on the thought of Thomas Aquinas in positing this specific scission between intellect and speech.[3] Taking some of Aquinas's comments as his model, Agamben draws a fine distinction between these two pillars of the medieval era:

> Here the philosopher clearly locates the process of learning in a double disjunction between the intellect and speech in which language exceeds the intellect (speaking without understanding) and the

intellect transcends language (understanding without speaking). While Thomas, however, limits himself to opposing two distinct and in every sense separate modes of learning (learning by discipline and learning by invention), Dante's genius consists in his having transformed the two into a double but nevertheless synchronous movement traversing the poetic act, in which invention is inverted into discipline (into listening) and discipline is inverted into invention, so to speak by virtue of its own insufficiency.[4]

Poetry is defined, as such, by a "constitutive disjunction between the intellect and language," one that appears only to have grown wider as time progressed into the modern era. Rather than shun this disjunction, poetry could itself be said to spring from this fracture—or inherent failure—within the subject, to express its origin as rooted in this ground. And rather than take such a state as a sign of complete failure, Agamben finds here the source of our creative, poetic endeavors:

> And is this not precisely what happens in every genuine poetic enunciation, in which language's movement toward sense is as if traversed by another discourse, one moving from comprehension to sound, without either of the two ever reaching its destination, the one to rest in prose and other in pure sound? Instead, in a decisive exchange, it is as if, having met each other, each of the two movements then followed the other's tracks, such that language found itself led back in the end to language, and comprehension to comprehension. This inverted chiasm—this and nothing else—is what we call poetry.[5]

Staking a great deal upon the origin of the poetic utterance, Agamben considers as beneficial to the poetic project the manner in which the fracture of our "human-being" is brought under measure and given description in language by poetry itself, and thereby he contemplates along with us why poetry is uniquely able to portray the failures of language to represent an object, any object. It is characteristic of poetry in all of this to be at a certain distance from itself in order to offer up this space to us—to *reflect* this space back to us. Poetry becomes, as such, an effort to distance our own words from their pronouncement, to step back and take account of the subject—which we also already are—as it is presented in the poem. As Robert Pinsky, a former poet laureate of the United States, has described this poetic activity elsewhere, "in its interior way the voice of poetry is like speaking, but also like watching oneself speak, from another terrain."[6] Again, this permanently exilic point of view, as both Rich and Celan confirm for us, is what actually allows the poet to navigate the ruins of language and to find the words to express our linguistic failures anew.

To return to the context of the medieval poets and the attention given to the element of the *corn* within the poem, poetry appears to Agamben as having been "traversed by a double tension, a tension that has its apex in the *corn*: one tension that seeks at every opportunity to split sound from sense, and another that, inversely, aims to make sound and sense coincide; one that attempts to distinguish the two wombs with precision, and another that wants to render the two absolutely indistinct."[7] Consequently, there is no easy distinction to make between sound and sense within a truly poetic utterance, and this fact is entirely characteristic of the poetic endeavor. Their paradox defines the existence of the poem, and despite the fact that this is a truth that threatens to undo the very nature of what we might consider the theological to be (as we will see in a moment), it is a truth to which theology has paid close attention in some regard throughout the ages. For, as we will see Agamben develop immediately within this context, "The extreme case is *glossolalia*, in which sense and sound cannot be told apart," a theological "gift" to some, and something that even the biblical account of its occurrence struggled to come to terms with representing.[8]

The Phenomenon of Glossolalia

It is no coincidence that the phenomenon of *glossolalia*, so interwoven with the fate of the poetic experience, should find its theological embodiment in the miraculous act of "speaking in tongues" found in the texts of the New Testament. Agamben's commentary upon this scriptural setting for the fundamental split between sound and sense is all the more appropriate to relate when considering the development of this general atheological enterprise—akin to what we have already seen in the work of Celan, and what I will explore in the writings of Saint Paul—as a phenomenon that might yet be discernable at the heart of scripture's own narratives. Indeed, Agamben's more recent reflections upon the nature of the theological, as well as his attempts to isolate a force of profanation within it, are indications of this continuous trajectory of his thoughts, questioning the sources of theology in order to provide a path toward the profanation of our world.[9] Amidst so many recent conjectures on the "atheological" elements latent within Pauline thought—Alain Badiou's and Jean-Luc Nancy's foremost among them—Agamben's early use of Paul's writings in relation to the poetic seems not only to confirm these intuitions, but actually to develop them still further, while also allowing us to see the essential role that the poetic plays in the construction of the a/theological.

To begin isolating this effect, it is in the midst of highlighting Paul's critique of "unknown tongues" in 1 Corinthians 14:1–25 that Agamben notes that the term *glossa* is to be understood as "speech foreign to the language of use; [an] obscure term, whose meaning is not understood." Taken together with the traditional Greek understanding that such a "gloss" is something of a "mysterious language" in itself, he speculates that glossolalia is "not the pure utterance of inarticulate sounds but rather a 'speech in glosses,' that is, a speech whose meaning is unknown, exactly like Augustine's *temetum* [intoxicating drink]."[10] This phenomenon appears later on in Paul's letters as a phenomenon simply barbaric to Paul, as to speak without knowing what one is saying—to not know the *dynamis* of the words themselves, as Agamben puts it—is to render their usage meaningless. In Paul's view of things, "To-speak-in-gloss is thus to experience in oneself barbarian speech, speech that one does not know; it is to experience an 'infantile' speech ('Brethren, be not children in understanding') in which understanding is 'unfruitful.'"[11] Such language is "unfruitful" because it is unknowable and seemingly worthless to those who hear its sound but are entirely unmoved by it, its meaning being simply dead to their ears.

Yet, for Agamben, there is also something else at work in the phenomenon of *glossolalia* that Paul both does and does not comprehend. What Paul sensed as operative within the phenomenon of glossolalia, but which he did not completely observe, was the potential to render language itself inoperative—a formulation that will echo deeply throughout Agamben's later writings. As he puts it in this context, "*Glossolalia* and *xenoglossia* are the ciphers of the death of language: they represent language's departure from its semantic dimension and its return to the original sphere of the pure intention to signify (not mere sound, but rather language and thought of the voice alone)."[12] Through the operations of glossolalia, language itself is exposed as a bare phenomenon as it were, the rift between sound and sense widened and revealed to the world that had once sought to sacramentalize its union.[13] A great deal of Agamben's later analysis of language and human action (manifest as both politics and ethics) will rest upon this observation.

Symbolically, these characterizations are important for discerning the path that poetry has taken and continues to take into the late-modern, or even postmodern world in relation to the establishment of the theological—a field itself founded, one might say, on the unity of sound and sense. From this point of view, we must take this relationship between poetry and theology seriously, especially if Agamben's analysis is to be considered as an attempt to go beyond the meaning inherently conveyed through the union of poetry and theology, aiming rather straight toward the existence of language itself—a point I will return to later in this chapter.

Certainly, for Agamben, the poet who has most readily accepted the poetic task of dealing with this loss of meaning in words—discernable already in the phenomenon of glossolalia—and therefore the reinvention of the a/theological, is the twentieth-century Italian poet Giovanni Pascoli, whose work proves inspirational to Agamben in more than one regard. Agamben notes, for starters, how Pascoli centers our thoughts on glossolalia by determining how "poetry, like religion, needs 'words that veil and darken their meaning, words, I mean, foreign to present use' (and which are nevertheless used 'to give greater life to thought')."[14] Remaining in a realm where a language's content seems lost, though its form remains visible, is an attempt to cross from the realm of the poetic experience of dictation to the philosophical experience of language, which—and as I will develop later in detail—is the trajectory of human experience that religion, he will suggest, has sought to obfuscate with its myriad attempts to define its own inner "mystical" workings, a claim that rests upon the sheer difficulty of expressing the existence of language. Yet if religion has had a particular historical task it has set for itself, it is this: to deal with the existence of language, a fact that cannot be pronounced as such *in* language and, therefore, must be treated as a sacrament of sorts, a reality best expressed through the historical use of oaths and creeds, statements intended to deal with such a state of our linguistic being.[15] For both poetry and philosophy, glossolalia illustrates an attempt to complete the journey from the one to the other, something that inherently invokes the difficulties and perplexities of crossing over an inconceivable threshold and invoking the dark void of death. For theology, glossolalia reveals the inner tension that motivates its raison d'être and thus is precisely why Paul's fascination with the phenomenon is so significant. "Poetry, Pascoli says, speaks in a dead language; but dead language is what gives life to thought. Thought lives off the death of words. From this perspective, to think and to poeticize is to experience the death of speech, to utter (and to resuscitate) dead words."[16]

What we encounter at this point in his commentary on Pascoli is a particular resonance with Saint Paul's writing in his Letter to the Romans on the experience of "dying with Christ" that is not coincidental to the overall tone Agamben wishes to set forth in the context of Pascoli's poetry. In fact, the theological tradition is immersed, though most often completely unknowingly, in an attempt to do exactly what Pascoli is attempting to do with his poetry, and they are both attempts that fail to achieve their goals independent of one another. To state but one recurring example of this coincidence between the poetic and the theological in action, Agamben turns from Pascoli to Saint Augustine, who, for his part, seems to have sensed something of the profundity of their proximity:

For Augustine, this experience of an unknown word (*verbum igno-tum*) in the no-man's-land between sound and signification is the experience of love as will to know. What corresponds to the intention to signify without signification is not logical understanding, in fact, but rather the desire to know (*qui scire amat incognita, non ipsa incognita, sed ipsum scire amat*: love is thus always the desire to know). It is important, however, to stress that the site of this experience of love, which shows the *vox* in its purity, is a dead word, a *vocabulum emortuum*: *temetum*.[17]

It is the experience of love in Augustine's eyes that is what poetry attempts to register and access for us, even if the poem is not recognizable as a traditional "love poem." As Agamben claims, this is what Guanilo, writing once in response to Saint Anselm, called the "thought of voice alone," an "unheard dimension sustained in the pure breath of the voice."[18]

Much as with his writings on love and the qualities of the beloved (as "whatever being"), Agamben seems to be gesturing toward a definition of love as what remains once all the effects to produce it have fallen away, as with his understanding of the existence of language beyond the tensions of sound and sense, or, elsewhere, as truth appears only in the failures of our representations.[19] At the base of these reflections, it becomes possible to see why Agamben would so often have recourse to the history of theology in the midst of his modern poetic formulations, for it is only through a diffusion of the theological into the fabric of our most basic (poetic) use of language that Agamben can point out the various (theological) ways put forth to "heal" the fracture at the heart of the relationship between poetry and philosophy, or that which has come to define the Western subject. The theological, he will claim, has always sought to resolve the tension between sound and sense, though it was not correctly perceived as trying to undertake such an effort. Once Agamben is able to demonstrate the reality of this quest, and its inherently theopoetic nature, he seeks to rest content with the unmasking of this futile endeavor, a realization that ultimately brings about his advocating an inherently *atheological* position.

With reference to Saint Augustine, Agamben describes how this zone of indistinguishability between sense and sound—captured in the experience of glossolalia—has historically been portrayed as "a zone of indifference, so to speak, between lived experience and what is poeticized, an 'experience of speech' as an inexhaustible experience of love."[20] In reality, an ontology of inexpressible love does appear in the space that poetry creates between the poem and the reader, and that seems to be supported by the way in which the nature of the theological has been defined throughout history. Reclaiming some ground from what theology has often exclusively sought to govern and from what poetry has sought to reassert in the modern world, Agamben demonstrates how this ontological reality (of love) takes root in the experience of the poet rather than of the theologian. An "experience of the dwelling of speech in the beginning" (comparable to the theological emphasis on the *logos* in creation), as well as a way to demonstrate how life is only that which is lived *in* speech, becomes available to the poet who subsequently creates and dwells within this space of love, though without any need of the theological. The philosophical experience of language, which seeks to understand the origins of language and which proceeds in an opposing direction, thereby provides a fitting compliment to the poetic experience.

The moment of coincidence between poetry and philosophy is consequently what enables Agamben to describe the essence of what constitutes the "poem" as such: "Poetry contains in fact an element that always already warns whoever listens or repeats a poem that the event of language at stake has already existed and will return an infinite number of times. This element . . . is the metrical-musical element."[21] That is, the very division of the poem itself, its spacing and meter spread out over time, is what gives the poem, according to Agamben, its priority and significance in disclosing the parameters of our linguistic being. It is what meets the philosophical arc stemming from the other side and pushing (traditionally, theologically) toward sense in order to establish the human subject. To see this operation for what it is—once justified theologically, but no longer needing this legitimation—is an authentic disclosure of something so necessarily internal to our being (like the sublimity of music) that it is often overlooked or neglected altogether—and *this* is Agamben's unique contribution to the study of what constitutes poetry, in the first place, as an atheological exercise. As he phrases it, "We are accustomed to reading poetry as if the metrical element had no importance from a semantic point of view. Certainly, it is said, metrical-musical structure is essential to a given poem and cannot be altered—but usually we do not know *why* it is so essential or what precisely it says in itself."[22] Its essence, then, is now revealed as the gathering of the self in an ontology of love, seemingly, *beyond* the sphere of language, yet accessible only *through* the fractured nature of the language of the poem. The reason for the poem's existence, as Agamben argues, is caught up in establishing the parameters (para-*meters* of sound and space, of sound through space) of human experience, both linguistic and not, and as such both theological and not. What transpires within the poetic act— in its mad flight toward sense—is much deeper in relation to the human being than the theological.

The verse (*versus*, from *verto*, the act of turning, to return, as opposed to *prorsus*, to proceed directly, as in prose) signals for a reader that these words have always already come to be, that they will return again, and that the instance of the word that takes place in a poem is, for this reason, ungraspable. Through the musical element, poetic language commemorates its own inaccessible originary place and it says the unspeakability of the event of language (*it attains*, that is, *the unattainable*).[23]

Though the word expressed in the poem remains ultimately "ungraspable," the poem nonetheless still testifies to its "inaccessible originary place," that which is the abyss from which language (*logos*) arises and in which, traditionally, the name of God was often held. In this way, the "unobtainable origin" behind the poem *can be* obtained in some sense, can be grasped though it had seemed unobtainable, and what can be grasped becomes the source of a profound potential for transformation. That is, our "failure" to grasp it becomes, in turn, the very locus of our creative inspiration. It is in the "as if" dimension of the poetic word that some *thing* perhaps becomes presentable *beyond* the words that represent it, present in the very failures of these words to represent anything at all. This is also where, as Agamben puts it, the "unnameable name" (*nomen innominabile*) of God becomes *perhaps* pronounceable, *as if* for the first time.[24]

Toward an Atheological Poetry

In this poetic discovery of a presence before us only glimpsed in the failure of our words and of our representations, there is an eclipse of the need for the theological that we would do well to note as a major component of Agamben's analysis. There are certainly intimations here of a pregrammatical language that poetry seeks to encounter (*the* space for love to occur), something found in the use of onomatopoeia, for example, and which again signals for Agamben a return to an originary state he terms our "infancy" (overlapping perhaps somewhat too with the "infantile" speech Paul had condemned glossolalia as sounding like).[25] Rather than exist as some Edenic paradise, however, the state of infancy he describes is one said to dwell beyond the realm of the theological altogether, existing as a realm of pure letters (*grammata*) that hold forth the *potential* to signify without yet signifying anything—again, a moment of sound without sense. To envision such a state would be akin perhaps to witnessing the face of the infant, which looks so often as if it is about to express something determinate while yet refraining from doing so, a site of "pure potentiality" which has not yet crossed over into actuality, and which holds the key in many ways to accessing the limitless creative potential within each of us.[26]

There is also locatable here an originary purity to such a gesture that Agamben is quick to portray as *the* truth after which theology has been so determinately seeking through its various formulations of grace over the centuries, and which it cannot yet completely articulate.[27] This precise location is likewise the site where Pascoli, for one, determined the relevance of his most basic poetic gestures, something that will direct Agamben's gaze more resolutely toward the atheological. In Agamben's commentary:

> The letter is therefore the dimension in which *glossolalia* and ono-matopoeia, the poetics of dead language and the poetics of the dead voice, converge in one site, where Pascoli situates the most proper experience of poetic dictation: *the site in which he can capture language in the instant it sinks again, dying, into the voice, and at which the voice, emerging from mere sound, passes (that is, dies) into signification.*[28]

This, as I have already stressed, is Agamben's true target: signification itself, the ultimate source of our various created boundaries of cultural significance.[29] The stakes of comprehending the significance of this definition of poetry are great for the modern subject (which we will see only heightened in a moment through the works of both Rilke and Caproni), especially as regards the life and determination of the a/theological subject—the subject legitimated by the a/theological.

Defining the Scission between Poetry and Philosophy

From Agamben's viewpoint, modernity lives under the sign of the destruction of experience, a very real and embodied confrontation with the failures of our world and of our representations. We are said to dwell in a context wherein the quotidian can no longer be translated into true experience and, where we, modern subjects, remain awash in a near useless sea of information. Following the lead of Walter Benjamin, for whom the debris of modernity and its attempts at historical progress are simply so much wreckage strewn across Western culture,[30] Agamben presents a similar analysis in setting the stage for the scission, or fracture, which traces itself through the foundations of the modern subject, and which very much constitutes the failures of representation I have been discussing thus far. The authority once present in our world that had previously guaranteed "the truth of an experience" has, likewise, waned to the point that events are now "non-translatable" into an authentic experience.[31] Experiences happen, but they do not happen to us, the touristic masses who would be more often likely to take a picture of an event than genuinely experience it.[32]

From Agamben's perspective, this lack of authentic experience is perhaps nowhere more adequately registered than in the field of modern poetry, for it "responds to the expropriation of experience by converting this expropriation into a reason for surviving and making the inexperiencible its normal condition."[33] Within modern poetry, the destruction of experience is portrayed with such a vivid accuracy that Agamben is often drawn to the images and metaphors that appear to ceaselessly collide in our culture and that could only be described as a "jumble of events" in which humanity now finds itself. However, it is also a jumble of events with which the poet is always contemporary.[34] Since authority today asserts itself on what cannot be experienced, he repeatedly claims,[35] modern poets would seem to register themselves as the ultimate authority in society (Shelley's "unacknowledged legislators") insofar as modern poetics attempts to reach out to the "inexperiencible."

In this state, the poet actually comes to *re*present this scission within identity through the images and metaphors that are emblematic of this condition. Our time, Agamben warns us, is characterized by a fracture within the subject of experience, a split that is uniquely captured by the figure of Don Quixote in relation to his sidekick, Sancho Panza, a comparison he evokes on occasion.[36] In Cervantes's masterwork, a work that almost singularly signaled the birth of the modern novel, Don Quixote, as protagonist, represents the "old subject of knowledge," capable of undergoing fantastic experiences without actually possessing them in reality. He pursues his fantasies without their ever converging with established social realities. Conversely, his sidekick, Sancho Panza, represents the "old subject of experience" and, accordingly, is only able to know the experience for what it is, that is, to expose the fantasy as not being reality but without actually undergoing an experience himself. It is only Don Quixote who can *have* the experience without *knowing* it and Sancho Panza who can *know* the reality without really *having* it. The comical, and yet tragic, paradox of the fractured existence that results is characteristic of what Agamben will call the scission between knowledge and experience—as earlier between sound and sense—a general division that comes to define the modern subject.

In the poetic writings of the late nineteenth and early twentieth centuries specifically, he finds that this scission resonates with an "awareness of an appalling expropriation of experience, of an unprecedented 'void of experience'" in the poetry of Rainer Maria Rilke, being but one, albeit major, example.[37] If Baudelaire could be said to be the poet who heralded the "destruction of the transmissibility of culture" in the modern era and thus was given over to focus on the "inexperiencible" within experience,[38] it is Rilke whom Agamben sees as resolutely, though contradictorily, trying to bridge the gap between the two. Characteristically refraining from any close analysis of poetic texts in favor of generalized reflections, Agamben maintains that it is a "void of experience" present in Rilke's work that also drains any sense of the "mystical" from inhabiting the poetic word, and concerns now only "the daily life of a citizen of the twentieth century,"[39] echoing in many ways Lacoue-Labarthe's earlier reading of Celan. *This* is the first mark, for Agamben, of an atheological poetry.[40] It is this poetic disclosure of our world in its nonmysticality that he furthers, and that allows him to state elsewhere that the mystical is not *in* language, but *is* language itself, thereby removing the possibility for any traditional mystical-transcendent formulations.[41] Modernity, by this count, has brought an end to any speculative, redemptive transcendence, a fact illustrating quite pointedly why certain twentieth century schools of thought, such as the New Critics, once thought that poetry had come to replace both religion and philosophy.

Agamben nonetheless sees Rilke's creative acts as suspended over an abyss separating knowledge from experience, though this is an abyss that is actually the internal fracture of a common source for our humanity, experienced as the dissonance present (its presence) between them. That is, the human being is constructed in this abyss or gap between our knowledge and our experience, a truth he will later take up in his reflections on the borders that he suggests *artificially* separate the human from the animal.[42] With regard to the poetic, we are told that "unlike Baudelaire and Rimbaud, who entrust humanity's new experience resolutely to the inexperiencible," Rilke himself can be said to oscillate:

> between two contradictory worlds. In the angel, the puppet, the acrobat and the child he holds up the figures of a *Dasein* which has totally freed itself from all experience; on the other hand, he evokes nostalgically the things in which individuals "accumulated the human" . . . and which were thereby made "liveable" and "sayable," in contrast to the "appearances of things" which "bear down from America" and have now transposed their existence "within the vibration of money."[43]

Drawing upon a Heideggerian conceptualization of *Dasein* (being-there), a precarious "thrown-ness" into a world wherein we feel a sense of alienation and dread,[44] Agamben analyzes Rilke's most thought-provoking and quasi-mystical work against the backdrop of a late-modern disintegration of the subject. Like those analyses that would link Heidegger to Celan, another poet for whom the traditional subject of poetry had died,[45] this disintegration of the subject serves to reveal nothing less than the total absence of transcendence in our world. As Agamben will describe things, "The fact of being suspended between these two worlds like one of the 'disinherited' . . . is the central experience of Rilke's poetry, which, like many works deemed esoteric, has no mysticism in it, but concerns the daily life of a citizen of the twentieth century."[46] The modern poet is truly therefore without a transcendent deity.

This lack of mysticism, as a crucial absence within the modern aesthetic form, makes Rilke's poetry central for Agamben in a way that Baudelaire cannot be, for to express the ineffable is no longer a transcendent, mystical proposition as it was for medieval theologians or for Dante; it is simply the origin (and existence) of language itself, a fact that language itself cannot express *in* language.[47] Rilke's suspension between these two worlds confirms, for Agamben, the fundamental split in the subject of experience, something he further develops in the contrast taken up between poetry and philosophy. There, we again have Don Quixote (this time representing poetry *as* experience) confronting his inseparable partner Sancho Panza (now philosophy *as* knowledge), a relationship that Rilke, according to Agamben, will at many points attempt to foster within his own work. In these reformulated though equivalent terms, the scission between poetry and philosophy posits a dichotomous realm of experience wherein poetry is seen as possessing its object without knowing it, and philosophy as knowing it without possessing it.[48] These two poles of experience come to exhibit a sort of symbiotic relationship that humanity undergoes in its constant attempt to articulate and justify its existence.

In essence, neither poetry nor philosophy can solely lead us toward an experience of the fullness of our humanity. This is so because "knowledge . . . is divided between inspired-ecstatic and rational-conscious poles, neither ever succeeding in wholly reducing the other."[49] Poetry must complete what philosophy cannot, and, perhaps this time, *together*, they can unite the poles of our knowledge, bringing us to the threshold of a prelinguistic (infantile) state beyond any subjection to language's hold.[50] Just as Agamben will later refer to Celan's poetry as a possible experience of a "nonlanguage," there is a realm of gesture beyond language that poetry points toward and that only philosophy can complete.[51] Rather than disdain the poetic, as Plato was wont to do in his original distinction between poetry and philosophy[52]—finding favor only with the latter and ousting the former from his Republic—Agamben finds some hope in their mutual interaction.[53]

This benefit, however, is a task that neither poetry nor philosophy has fully entertained in the modern period (especially insofar as it was only the theological that could once guarantee any sort of unity on this score). As Agamben continues the analysis, he is critically constructive of their interaction: "Insofar as philosophy and poetry have passively accepted this division, philosophy has failed to elaborate a proper language, as if there could be a royal road to truth that would avoid the problem of its representation, and poetry has developed neither a method nor self-consciousness."[54] Their sharing of the object of experience is for this reason often missed, resulting in a further fragmentation of experience in the modern world. Humanity continues to fail in its efforts for authenticity, continues to fail in uniting the objects of what both disciplines search for: "What is thus overlooked is the fact that every authentic poetic project is directed toward knowledge, just as every authentic act of philosophy is always directed toward joy."[55] Taken together, poetry and philosophy seek to complete both the knowledge and joy of humanity. Lacking either, any alleged fullness repeatedly dwindles, allowing further scissions, as well as an accompanying sense of alienation, to dominate.

Like philosophy, which earlier faced the abyss from which language (*logos*) itself arises, poetry too faces "the negative experience of the place of language that we encountered as fundamental in the Western philosophical tradition."[56] As Agamben will elsewhere elaborate on this shared trajectory of poetry and philosophy, we have here two partners who must, like Don Quixote and Sancho Panza, complete their quest together, and despite their conflicting views of reality, because *both* efforts are attempts to wrestle with our establishment of the human being in the face of the existence of language, a reality with which we have not yet learned to deal, and this despite what theology had once managed to accomplish. It is their common negative experience, the abyss that they share in relation to language, which "while separating them, also holds them together and seems to point beyond their fracture."[57] It is this fact of the existence of language, an event beyond the "mystical" because so *thoroughly material*, which both philosophy and poetry seek to reveal. Indeed, accepting language's existence as the ultimate reality with which we struggle is, for Agamben, truly a "revelation."[58]

Traits of the poetic, in this fashion, become parallel formulations of the philosophical and vice versa—their shared heritage in reacting to the abyss of language dictating that it be so. Ontology, and, in a Heideggerian sense, its accompanying ontotheological justifications, are to be understood as *what takes place* in the relationship between the two, the alleged "true human language" that should otherwise appear in the coming together of poetry and philosophy.[59] Previously seen as *the* fundamental study of our being, ontology is now capable of being perceived as little more than an often-failing attempt to bridge the gap between poetry and philosophy, or between the human and the animal, the two most radical experiments ever conceived in trying to overcome the hold of language. Consequently, Agamben finds a deep resonance, or a "perfect coincidence," between the "poetic experience of dictation" and the philosophical experience of language. Though the latter has often been seen as a discerner of ontological forms, the former has been kept aloof from such pronouncements, left to toil under the complete rule of metaphor.

Concerning poetic dictation—and here echoing a good deal of the analysis already made concerning his take on the poetic in other contexts—Agamben explains how the foundations of poetry are marked by the experience of a dictation that is "neither a biographical nor a linguistic event."[60] It is instead something inherent to the poetic experience, a (formal) rhythm or rhyme *that makes an ontological claim of its own*, apart from any potential ontological claims made on behalf of an alleged subject produced through acts of linguistic signification. This is why poetry matters for Agamben in a way that it did not for Plato: an "experience of the dwelling of speech in the beginning," (comparable, for him, to a theological emphasis on the *logos* found within creation), as a way to demonstrate how life is only that which is lived in speech, becomes an experience available to the poet who creates this space for being to appear. Philosophy, for its part, may bring us a method and self-consciousness for understanding our ontological forms, but it cannot clear the space for these forms to dwell. It is poetically, as Hölderin once put it, that humanity dwells, and Agamben, for his part, wishes to highlight this apparent truth with renewed force. Hence, the philosophical experience of language, which seeks to understand the origins of language itself, and which proceeds from the opposite direction, provides a fitting compliment to the poetic experience, though it cannot accomplish what poetry ultimately can. Their tasks remain separate, though equally necessary in this regard.

Like his later comments on the importance of testimony, or the saying of the *unsaid* in every *said*,[61] Agamben turns to the poetic utterance in order to ground an aspect of human existence beyond *the said*. Only in poetry, we are told, and if we are prepared to accept it, can the "unnameable name" of God become perhaps pronounceable.[62] This is the case because, though the word expressed in the poem remains ultimately "ungraspable," the poem nonetheless still testifies to its "inaccessible originary place"—again, the abyss from which language (*logos*) arises and in which the name of God could be said to dwell. Only somewhat "theologically," it would seem, can the "unobtainable origin" behind the poem be obtained, though it will be, in the end, a "theological" effort best construed as "atheological."

What becomes clear through this tracing of the interaction between poetry and philosophy is that the realm of the theological has existed historically, for Agamben, as an attempt to state the "mystical" unity of poetry and philosophy, the "unpronounceable" origin which connects them and which remains unstated in all that they express. This is what will make the majority of our ontological statements, as potential bridges between the two, always already ontotheological. As this linkage between the object which poetry and philosophy seek to unify and the name of God illustrates, Agamben turns often, in this context, to the sphere of divine and human religious experiences, as well as the theological and biblical traditions that record them. In essence, theological motifs appear to him as saturated with the quest to frame our search for origins, which is synonymous with the quest for a prelinguistic (infantile) realm. Religion is framed by him as an attempt *to be* the solution to the fracture between poetry and philosophy, *to be* in fact that perfect language that unites their disparate quests.

From Greek mythology to Judeo-Christian scripture, the search for language to which both poetry and philosophy attest becomes the quasi-mystical endeavor that religion indeed mistakes as the mystical, ineffable source of all divinity.[63] What is truly revealed, in actuality, then, is not a transcendent deity waiting on the other side of things, but the unspeakable fact of our linguistic origins, of language itself, that it exists in the first place but cannot be stated as such in any pure manner. As he puts it:

> That which is construed as the supreme mystical experience of being and as the perfect name of God . . . is the experience of the meaning of the *gramma* itself, of the letter as the negation and exclusion of voice. . . . As the unnameable name of God, the *gramma* is the final and negative dimension of meaning, no longer an experience of language but language itself, that is, its taking place in the removal of the voice.[64]

Not only is this vision of language and theology one that he inherited from Benjamin, who had previously sought to discern a "divine language" beyond our human ones, it is a fact of our linguistic existence to which both poetry and philosophy point.[65] It *is* the material essence of what constitutes the theological tout court. This "purely theological presupposition" is what, in another context, he describes as "the dwelling of the word in the beginning, of *logos* in *archē*, that is, the absolutely primordial status of language."[66] It is for this reason, I would further speculate, that theology has become almost *the* central focus of Agamben's work over recent years.[67] Theology discloses an inadvertent truth about the origin of language that is yet entirely material, and it is this truth which Agamben has become particularly attuned to, that which he seeks to disclose as an entirely *profane* revelation—and which, again, shares a good deal in Lacoue-Labarthe's reading of Celan's poetry.

In what is still the most comprehensive assessment of Agamben's work to date, Leland de la Durantaye has charted the progression of Agamben's poetics as it merges with his general comments on the destruction of experience in the modern era (and the accompanying de-subjectification of the subject) and as it is for Agamben an attempt to isolate the "Idea of Language."[68] What Durantaye refrains from overtly pronouncing, however, is how Agamben's understanding of poetry not only refers back to his earlier work on aesthetics,[69] which Durantaye *does* point out, but that it also points directly to theological themes within his more recent writing. This is something we would do well not to overlook, as Agamben is attempting to expose the theological grounding of both disciplines as a purely immanent, material domain, one concerned with our inability to express our linguistic origins. As he sets the stage for it in yet another context: "This uninterrogated persistence of a theological foundation shows itself in the fact that the original structure of the poetic work remains marked by negativity: the primordiality of *logos* thus quickly becomes a primacy of the signifier and the letter, and the origin reveals itself as trace."[70] It is a trace that has frequently (and traditionally) been intuited as the divine murmur working within our world. For Agamben, as he later re-emphasizes throughout his work on the apostle Paul, it is also the Christian legacy that has uniquely disseminated this principle of language's origin.[71]

In reference to the prologue of John's Gospel, for example, Agamben states: "Life is what is made in speech and what remains indistinguishable from it and close to it. This unquestioned bond of speech and life is the inheritance that Christian theology transmits to a literature that has not yet become fully profane."[72] The conclusion Agamben has been subtly working toward, I would suggest at this point, is the realization of the true task of poetry and philosophy apart from theology's efforts to unite them: a full pronouncement of humanity's (prelinguistic) origins. That is, they both seek to dissolve any semblance of the theological and to realize the potentiality latent behind its otherwise transcendent (sovereign) statements. The ontotheological legacy that exists as an attempt to suture the scission between poetry and philosophy must be discarded, and theology will never be the same again.[73]

The Further Development of an A/Theological Poetry

It is intriguing, though not coincidental, that Agamben's remarks concerning the search for a true "human language" beyond the theological will ultimately discover their reflection in a work written decades later, where his attentions have turned directly to the apostle Paul. There, Agamben discerns how Paul's contribution to Western poetic thought was an unparalleled messianic rhythm that became a poetic dictation pointing toward the origin of the *logos*, or Paul's Christ. To see things as such is to see the inseparability of the poem's form (its rhythm/rhyme) from its content (its sound from its sense), something that is likewise disclosed in Paul's declarations of messianic time. His study on Paul thus ends with this hypothesis: "rhyme, understood in the broad sense of the term as the articulation of a difference between semiotic series and semantic series, is the messianic heritage Paul leaves to modern poetry, and the history and fate of rhyme coincide in poetry with the history and fate of the messianic announcement."[74] Again seeking to eradicate any traces of the theological which would otherwise seek to introduce a misleading, and in the end unhelpful, notion of transcendence into our world, Agamben conceives of rhyme as entirely indebted to a particular theological legacy, and yet, because of its subsequent profane trajectory in his hands, as seemingly becoming an *atheological* device at the same time.

Though Agamben does not himself provide this connection, his comments on Paul's formulation of rhyme seem to be synonymous with his earlier discussion of rhythm in another context, and which might here help us to discern why the nature of rhyme/rhythm is so essential to an alternate conceptualization of time.[75] In fact, the overlap between rhyme and rhythm seems most beneficial, for "Rhythm grants men both the ecstatic dwelling in a more original dimension and the fall into the flight of measurable time."[76] Rhythm, as fundamental to the poetic process, and as intertwined with poiesis, the act of creation, which lies at the origin of all art, is the theological legacy displaced into the sphere of the profane. The work of art is inextricably ordered in relation to its epochality, the fundamental rhythm from which it originates. As such, truth and history are conceived and, thereby, *revealed*. Rhythm presents to the individual an "authentic temporal dimension," and, at the same time, "the work of art also opens for him the space of his belonging to the world, only within which he can take the original measure of his dwelling on earth and find again his present truth in the unstoppable flow of linear time."[77] This, according to Agamben, is the truth that Paul revealed within the workings of the *logos*, within the messianic time that remained and that was always only something to be profaned.

Through the consideration of these remarks, we are able to make a profound connection between Paul's reworking of our understanding of time and the situation in which modern humanity finds itself most visibly within the poetic experience: we can conceive of poetry as an ecstatic experience that sets us outside of time-as-history's normal rhythm. In what appears mostly as a rather Heideggerian aesthetic formulation, Agamben is, therefore, able to state that:

> Man has on earth a poetic status, because it is *poiesis* that founds for him the original space of his world. Only because in the poetic ἐποχή he experiences his being-in-the-world as his essential condition does a world open up for his action and his existence. Only because he is capable of the most uncanny power, the power of pro-duction into presence, is he also capable of praxis, of willed and free activity. Only because he attains, in the poetic act, a more original temporal dimension is he a historical being, for whom, that is, at every instant his past and future are at stake.[78]

Poetry as *poiesis*, the act of creation posited through metaphor, transitions from the abyss of language to the instantiation of sin, and then from redemption to our infancy once again. Mimicking the cycle of philosophy, poetry's obverse partner in discovering the fullness of human existence, poetry returns to its point of origin, completing the necessary path of redemption and moving away from the snares of a state of original sin.[79] Just as philosophy sought to reveal the nature of our linguistic being, so too does poetry, but in a different way: to go beyond it as it were, and thus to re-enter into it from another angle. Poetry, it could be said, presents to us an experience of time outside the bounds of history and thus presents us with a privileged access to our existence beyond our constructed notions of what it means to be "human." Poetry and philosophy *together* complete the human experience that is otherwise fractured and incapable of rendering a presentation of itself, because they have been wedded to the various formulations of history that continue to dominate our representations of ourselves. The split we have been illuminating throughout is one not only between knowledge and experience, but one internal to our understanding of time itself.

Like T. S. Eliot's startling image of "The Hollow Men" within a modern landscape, looking to negotiate between the idea and the reality,[80] Agamben envisions a desolate humanity struggling to come to grips with its modern embodiment. Yet, rather than view this immense scission of the modern subject as one completely devoid of any meaning, as an abstract nihilism bent on eradicating all meaning in society, it can rather be seen as a radical reappropriation of our humanity, a profanation of what was once a sacred ground in-between the poetic and the philosophical. Poetry, rather than simply record the various states and tones of our struggles with our own humanity, actually illustrates the way out of this divided house. As Agamben puts it:

> Fetish or grail, site of an epiphany or a disappearance, it [poetry] reveals and once again dissolves itself in its own simulacrum of words until the program of alienation and knowledge, of redemption and dispossession, entrusted to poetry over a century ago by its first lucid devotees, will be accomplished.[81]

Poetry becomes an atheological enterprise because it must reinvent the way in which theology has been understood from its inception as an attempt to speak the truth of language's origin, a truth that, as we have seen, language itself cannot state. What theology has failed to do, poetry, in recognition of its failure to accurately represent anything, tries to accomplish. Citing Hölderlin's alteration of the line "as long as the god is not absent" to "as long as God's absence aids" in his poem "Dichterberuf" as the start of a poetic atheology, Agamben makes clear that it is not simply a "new theology" that Hölderin is after. Again carefully stressing what this movement is *not*, Agamben states:

> What begins here . . . is not a new theology; and it is not even a negative theology. . . . Nor is it an atheistic Christology . . . Hölderin's correction marks the point at which the divine and the human alike are ruined, at which poetry opens onto a region that is uncertain and devoid of a subject, flattened on the transcendental, and which can be defined only by the Hölderlinian euphemism, "betrayal of the sacred."[82]

Holding fast to these distinctions is not, for Agamben, a mere matter of clarifying genres; it is the determination of our subjectivity entirely without its ontotheological supports. This would be a subjectivity beyond those of our epoch that are continuously dismantled, rejoined, ill-fitted, and, contrary to what we had perhaps expected, beyond "Hölderin's half-god, Kleist's marionette, Nietzsche's Dionysius, the angel and the doll in Rilke, Kafka's Odradek, as well as Celan's 'Medusa-head' and 'automaton' and Montale's 'pearly snail's trace.'"[83] These are the fragmented figures upon the margins of our recognizable social and cultural representations that, for Agamben, speak loudly of the excluded figures from our political and cultural worlds, the various *homines sacri* that characterize his most salient political articulations.[84] The figures pushed to the limits of their humanity are here given a poetic voice, one strong enough to grant us a "transcendental orientation."[85] And yet, "What characterizes poetic atheology as opposed to every negative theology is its singular coincidence of nihilism and poetic practice, thanks to which poetry becomes the laboratory in which all known figures are undone and new, parahuman or semi-divine creatures emerge."[86] These figures signal the demise of the traditional theological methods used to justify the modern subject's integrity, but they also point us toward a radical potentiality within our existence that could be described as an almost profane spirituality found through embracing our failures to represent the world as we would otherwise want to.

Though many of these figures have, at times, occupied a prominent position in Agamben's work as models of a peculiar modern experience of a subject's fragmentation, it is another poet who perhaps best embodies the contours that Agamben seeks to delineate in Hölderin's work and who frames the entirety of this atheological project. It is in the poetry of Giorgio Caproni that Agamben finds a poetic atheology that is "in flight beyond every familiar figure of the human and the divine."[87] This is a poetic atheology, according to Agamben, presented as the celebration of a fragmentation that has characterized modern poetry since Hölderin and the death of the closed metrical form.[88] Caproni's is a poetry that undoes the theological insofar as it reads theology against itself in order to more fully pronounce the "name of God" at the base of our quest to state the existence of language.

Caproni's poetry, in Agamben's eyes, introduces us to a "solitude without God," including, as Agamben summarizes it, the experience of the freedom to believe in God while knowing that there is no God,[89] as well as "a casual stopping point from which it is impossible to turn back, a trip leading nowhere and, at the same time, in flight beyond every familiar figure of the human and the divine."[90] As we might suspect, though not perhaps as Caproni would have had it, Agamben locates this poetry as being formed within a zone of pure potentiality that is opened through Caproni's poetic work, one in which humanity can finally locate something of its true nature.[91] As one of Agamben's most clearly delineated philosophical terms, a space of "pure potentiality" becomes one wherein a regression of sorts takes place beyond the "human being" typically constructed in the abyss between knowledge and experience.[92] With an atheological poetry, there is a movement backward into the potential that humanity holds, an almost undefinable experience of creative force beyond our normal cultural constructs. It is what, in the context of Caproni's poetry, Paolo Bartoloni portrays as an interstitial space created by the poetic experience, a space of being always between other spaces—a space that, even though it defies traditional groundings (or narratives) of the subject, has become the illustrious norm among contemporary novelists and poets, something Bartoloni locates in the writings of Giorgio Caproni, Italo Calvino, Vittorio Sereni, and Italo Svevo, to name but a few. As Bartoloni himself describes it, the interstitial space is the "only possible way to maintain intact the real presence of the object," yet it is also "to blind oneself to any images of it and experience it as potential and unknown, located in the interstitial space of a possible reality."[93] It is the experience of situating oneself between the dynamic tension of the poetic and the philosophical without ever having recourse to the (onto)theological in order to justify one's existence, or to grant oneself a sense of sovereign being.[94] It is not an experience of the inexperiencible, as one finds in Baudelaire, for example, but rather a poetic openness to the "whatever" nature of any singular creature before us.[95]

In such a fashion, Agamben's embrace of a poetic atheology allows him to reread theology (and ethics) anew. Hence, it is from the rich traditions of the mystics and Cabalists that Agamben draws a formulation of divine potentiality that runs counter to the sovereign images of God that have thus far dominated the history of theology, and that awakens us to a new potential for a theology as *a*theology, or a "theology without theology" in Derrida's terms—or what I would suggest is a theology willing to embrace its own hollow center, let go of its claims to (sovereign) power, and embrace its poverty or weakness.

In this poetic reformulation of God's power, it is God's descent into the "abyss" of God's own potentiality and impotentiality that brings forth creation, something that Agamben will explicitly link to the poetic, imaginative power of humanity to do likewise:

> In this context "abyss" is not a metaphor. As Jakob Böhme clearly states, it is the life of darkness in God, the divine root of Hell in which the Nothing is eternally produced. Only when we succeed in sinking into this Tartarus and experiencing our own impotentiality do we become capable of creating, truly becoming poets. And the hardest thing in this experience is not the Nothing or its darkness, in which many nevertheless remain imprisoned; the hardest thing is being capable of annihilating this Nothing and letting something, from Nothing, be.[96]

There is a radical continuum established between the immanent world filled with poetic tasks and the world that theology would claim on the other side of our linguistic existence. They are worlds, however, so completely interwoven that they structurally mirror each other, often provoking comments from Agamben that sound eerily like theological speculations, though his claim is that, in truth, they are the furthest thing from it. What we have, in the end, is something like a state wherein God's creative acts find their only proper reflection in our creative acts—if we allow ourselves to see it as such, that is, if we reside in the same pure potentiality wherein God was once said to dwell but now wherein we see only ourselves.

The Search for a Potential Meaning

> After one has abandoned a belief in god, poetry is that essence which takes its place as life's redemption.
>
> Wallace Stevens[97]

As Adorno once famously commented, "to write a poem after Auschwitz is barbaric."[98] In the face of such genocidal madness, how could one pretend as if aesthetics could construct our humanity as it had before. Later, of course, Adorno appeared to rescind such a claim by writing that "Perennial suffering has as much right to expression as a tortured man has to scream; hence it may have been wrong to say that after Auschwitz you could no longer write poems."[99] But the problematic remains: how are we to conceive of the poetic "after Auschwitz," after the "death of God" or the "death of the subject," as well as the political implications that flow from such questions?[100] How is poetry ever to be the same?

There is little doubt that poets are now poets of "destitute times," as Heidegger once phrased it, searching for a way to move beyond the loss of the theological voice that formerly sustained humanity's quest to establish itself in poetry.[101] The trick, it would seem, is to keep the space between poetry and philosophy—once occupied by a theology established *as* ontology that was determined to reign sovereign within this space—*perpetually open*, without a specific identity, and without any sense of sovereign being that had previously characterized it. This is to leave the question of what makes us human a truly unanswerable one. That is, it is to leave, as Celan once attempted to do, the question of "Who?" permanently suspended, as Lacoue-Labarthe put it.[102] This, in the end, may be the only way to assure our world of a sense of meaning despite the loss of what had once (transcendently) appeared to hold us together.

Perhaps, by seeing things thus, we are poised to grant an answer to the question that Agamben asks often both directly and indirectly in his work: *Why does poetry matter to us?* If the theological is eclipsed by that which is immanent to it, its atheological potentiality, then the focus of so many historical desires becomes that pulse of life that poetry presents to us.[103] Though a romantic tendency would conceive of poetry as *being-one* with life itself and a secularist tendency would otherwise separate them completely, Agamben, alternatively, perceives of poetry as united *with* life *in* the medium of language. With this formulation, he is able to maintain their separateness in terms of the biography and psychology of the individual subject, but also their "becoming indistinct at the point of their reciprocal desubjectivization."[104] That is, they are most nearly aligned when the subject, as is the case with the poet, finds the self unraveling—when it confronts its own failures as potential sources of a creative, albeit *profaned*, spirituality. This is so because the poet "is he who, in the word, produces life."[105] It is this creative imprint which the poet leaves that signals a movement away from an overemphasized personal subjectivity and toward the pulse of life itself, an animality of the human being beyond the human subject: "Life, which the poet produces in the poem, withdraws from both the lived experience of the psychosomatic individual and the biological unsayability of the species."[106] Or, we might say, *life lives of its own accord*, and the privileged poet is able—if even only for a brief while—to take part in its processes and forget about the subject that the poet was traditionally conditioned to be. This is to introduce poetry in the modern age as nothing less than a completely atheological project that is yet somehow theological as well, as I have been contending throughout this chapter—perhaps what William Watkin has referred to as poetry's capacity "to save metaphysics from itself."[107]

The life that is lived over and beyond any conceivable notion of subjectivity (i.e., of the political, cultural, or religious subject) is likewise capable of traversing the traditional terrain of how humanity has defined itself, producing a new anthropology of the subject as an essentially poetic task. As Agamben answers the question of poetry's significance:

> [P]oetry matters because the individual who experiences this unity in the medium of language undergoes an anthropological change that is, in the context of the individual's natural history, every bit as decisive as was, for the primate, the liberation of the hand in the erect position or, for the reptile, the transformation of limbs that changed it into a bird.[108]

These are, of course, extremely significant alterations in self-understanding, from the biological to the theological, and back again (to an atheological *life*). Yet this is also how Agamben, for example, is able to say that poetry can become the point where nature is indistinguishable from grace, dwelling from gift, or possession from expropriation.[109] It is a world bereft of its traditional theological contents and better off for it, more open to the presentation of the other before us and more open to a complete reformulation of something like a "spirituality." This is an act of envisioning a world without signification as such and without the representations that reduce humanity through the violence they enact upon it.[110] The anthropology that Agamben is attempting to describe is one that is completely profaned, residing in a zone of indistinction between nature and grace, devoid of its previous religious justifications, an atheology *as* anthropology formed *through* the poetic enterprise and comprehended *in* the poetic experience. As Agamben sees it, poetry discloses an absolutely profane terminus, the true task given to humanity in remaining faithful to its roots, and established as an atheological enterprise that poetry cannot any longer cease to recognize as its own task.

In viewing poetry this way, we are able to reconceive of philosophy's task anew, for, once again, the two move in relation to one another, and, together, bring the human subject back to its originary fracture. In his own words, Agamben seeks to realize this task as a profound summons emanating from within. As he asks, "Are we capable of reckoning with the poetic presentation of the vocation that, as a nonpresupposed principle, emerges only where no voice calls us?"[111] Whereas theology had once attempted to fill in the gap separating art from myth with its messianic proclamations, and promised to deliver humanity from the scission at its core, poetry, in its ephemeral presentation of the split itself, offers another way to encounter the human being, one *beyond* theology, unique in its ability to simultaneously create a new sense of the theological entirely.[112]

There is a "self-liberation" possible for Agamben in the recognition of the scission, one that undoes the theological tradition, or any tradition, that would bar access to this potential for self-liberation. Accordingly, the presuppositions of theology, not to mention their hold over various traditional representations of the subject, are exposed by the uncovering of the inexpressible origin of language, the key to the dissolution of the "mystical" aura which surrounds religious traditions. Rather than being merely theological, or simply religious, "The fulfillment of the form of presupposition [through pronouncing language's origin in the inexpressible] and the decline of the power of representation [subsequently embraced through this fact now known] imply a poetic task and an ethical decision."[113] Quoting Celan to conclude his essay—and reminiscent of Ezra Pound's dictum that poetry should present and not represent[114]—Agamben states: "Poetry no longer imposes itself; it exposes itself."[115]

As Agamben has commented elsewhere, the caesuras within poetry make representation itself visible or manifest and, in turn, express the inexpressible through their presentation of the fracture within language (and being) itself.[116] In this sense, the only responsible way that a representation can be said to "present" truth is by illustrating the gap, or the caesura, that separates representation from truth itself.[117] If this is taken into consideration with what Agamben develops in another context as a form of "being-contemporary," we are left to witness the reality of how "the poet, insofar as he is contemporary, *is* this fracture, *is* at once that which impedes time from composing itself and the blood that must suture this break or this wound."[118] Embodying a radical vocation, the poet sits at a juncture in history wherein his or her experience is capable of expressing a profound sense of what Wallace Stevens once referred to as "life's redemption."[119]

Quite possibly we are now in a better position to comprehend Agamben's fascination with the work of Saint Paul, for whom the fracture within our being, theologically registered for him as "sin," was paramount to discovering our vocation before God. Paradoxical as it might appear for someone intent on disclosing the atheological nature of the poetic, it is by moving closer to Paul's theology that Agamben has hoped to illustrate the absolute distance which the poetic experience maintains in relation to what is traditionally considered as the domain of the "mystical-theological." Hence he can assert with full confidence that, in relation to this poetic sense of "being-contemporary," precedence is granted to the notion of a messianic realignment of time, one fully espoused in the Pauline corpus. As he puts it: "There is nothing more exemplary, in this sense, than Paul's gesture at the point in which he experiences and announces to his brothers the contemporariness par excellence that is messianic time, the being-contemporary with the Messiah, which he calls precisely the 'time of the now.'"[120] In this sense, it is the time of the poet as well, the time in which the fracture is exposed and therefore most open to the potential for its healing, though a healing that need not rely upon its traditional theological moorings. This would dictate, as well, the close proximity which the theological must maintain with the poetic and with one's access to love—at the same point wherein it appears to be completely lost to us in an atheological movement.

On more than one occasion, therefore, he has taken the time to elaborate upon Paul's relationship to poetry and the various implications that unfold from this analysis for humanity.[121] As he sees it, the poem is like the *katechon* in Paul's writings, "something that slows and delays the advent of the Messiah, that is, of him who, fulfilling the time of poetry and uniting its two eons, would destroy the poetic machine by hurling it into silence."[122] For, if poetry is only able to expose the rift in the subject, it is no one but the Messiah who demarcates the possibility of eradicating the rift, and thus poetry, altogether.

So, why, then, does the traditional domain of theology not allow the poetic to cross over on its own? Agamben seems to be asking this very question, perhaps in order to make the purely immanent merger between sound and sense a reality. As he frames the most pressing question in this regard, "what could be the aim of this theological conspiracy about language? Why so much ostentation to maintain, at any cost, a difference that succeeds in guaranteeing the space of the poem only on condition of depriving it of the possibility of a lasting accord between sound and sense?"[123] No matter the answer, it is a conspiracy that Agamben wishes to see to its end. But instead of this being an end wherein a theological word resonates within history, it is, rather, a profound silence—its own peculiar atheological essence—wherein humanity hears its own echo:

> [T]he poem falls by once again marking the opposition between the semiotic and the semantic, just as sound seems forever consigned to sense and sense returned forever to sound. The double intensity animating language does not die away in a final comprehension; instead it collapses into silence, so to speak, in an endless falling. The poem thus reveals the goal of its proud strategy: to let language finally communicate itself, without remaining unsaid in what is said.[124]

And if the poem can alone bring us to this threshold, then the task traditionally accorded to theology, and its ability to make a sacrament of language, is no longer necessary. What may, however, yet be possible, is a theology *beyond* this more traditional theology, one remaining to be written.

Consequently, an ethical paradigm is opened up through the exposition of the poem, one that calls us beyond the realm of representation and into the absolutely irreducible singularity of the particular person (as illustrated in the poetic gesture) before us. It is in this fashion that Agamben's formulation of an ethics of the face, an ethics that respects the singularity of the person before us, absent of all violent representations we would otherwise impose upon it, is thoroughly merged with his poetics.[125] The resulting *a*theological poetics is, no doubt, a bold stroke upon the canvas of the history of thought itself, a presentation of the self "beyond representation" and an attempt to redefine our most basic anthropological insights. It is also a challenge to the discipline of theology proper that it must now either reconcile itself to, reinventing itself along the way, or, as Agamben here demonstrates through his use of the theological tradition, risk being severed from itself forever.

Conclusion
The Spiritual and Creative Failures of Representation, or On the Art of Writing

"Perhaps" is a certain *anarche* that issues not in a street-corner anarchism or violent lawlessness, but in a radical, creative, and even sacred anarchy. Our lives are inscribed within a bottomlessness that no theoretical eye can fathom, in virtue of which we are ever exposed to time and tide and chance. What exists is neither protected from on high nor consigned to evil or violence or to a monstrous abyss that will swallow us whole like a tragic fate. What exists is inscribed within an aleatory element, exposed to an unavoidable chance and contingency which keeps the future open and unfinished. As a spacing, which is necessarily a disjointedness, "perhaps" is a way to confess that what is built up can in principle always be unbuilt, which is why things contain their own auto-deconstructibility. That is not nihilism but the condition of our lives, the condition of being created, and the chance of future creativity. That is the chance for grace.

—John Caputo[1]

At the end of this book, I am well aware that there is no systematic or formal way to conclude it. What I mean by this is that any effort to conclude the various strands of thought I have been pursuing throughout would be counterproductive to the point I have wished to make all along. I want, rather, to "end" this work with a more constructive project, to put some "flesh" on things a bit, and to point toward a concrete spirituality that these aesthetic reflections inspire. Perhaps, by sensing that all these reflections on the failures of our representations must have an effect upon one's self-representation as a writer, as an artist or poet even, those immersed in the processes I refer to here as the spiritual and creative failures of representation. If Agamben's examination of the a/theological subject within modernity is to have any weight behind it, I believe it might benefit us a good deal to try and examine what such a process might be for the writer as poet today.

For example, there are a number of ways I could have begun this conclusion, each one as contingent as the next, linking one phrase or concept to another, and then to another one, starting a chain of connections that tries to achieve its own inner integrity. My ability to recognize this absolute contingency of all writing—but, nonetheless, to still commit some words to a certain order and to move forward from that place—will in fact characterize the process of writing I will refer to throughout this conclusion, though it is something that certainly lingers underneath the entire book, as a practice of the "pure potentiality" of writing, drawing from Agamben's work what I take to be his most salient, concrete, and even practical point.

Within this process, the goal of the author, as paradoxical as it first appears to us, is to avoid creating a finished or actualized product, something that Derrida's work has testified to for quite some time. In this embracing of the potential over the actual, there is no *product* at all really, only the ongoing *processes* that never cease articulating and rearticulating themselves. This is where true thought is locatable, though never contained, as it pulses and maneuvers under everything that is said or written. Agamben himself has described this state: "Contrary to the traditional idea of potentiality that is annulled in actuality, here we are confronted with a potentiality that conserves itself and saves itself in actuality. Here potentiality, so to speak, survives actuality and, in this way, *gives itself to itself*."[2]

What exactly is this space of potentiality that I am speaking of, and that I believe Agamben has spoken of? How is it to be not just conceptualized but embodied? And how might such an embodiment help us to reformulate our various historical notions of spirituality, or what I take to be the interconnectedness of the failures of our representations—the only real "presentations" of the selves that we all are?

At least initially, I believe we must consider it as space as liminal and flexible as one might come to expect of it—it is as contingent as anything else that exists, making it, surely, difficult for many to comprehend. In terms of creative expression, it allows the author as poet—as the example I intend to take up here—to make sense of the methods they employ each time they sit down to compose a piece of writing. That is, it contextualizes entirely the processes they undertake the moment they sit down to write. The writer thus starts wherever they start, in the middle or at the end, perhaps simply with a series of incomplete fragments that link together in ways often unclear at first. From these multiple potential points of origin, the writer slowly begins to make connections and to expand and correct, contract and revise. The process takes its own course, much as a river flows with the landscape, and the author sometimes least of all knows where it is heading in the end. The best that can be said is that the writer tries to direct things as best as they can, though mostly very poorly and with a sense that they cannot really steer things where they would like them to be. They are, mostly, simply along for the ride in this sense, moving erratically backward and forward, jumping at times far ahead or far behind, and often at a seemingly random pace.

These are spaces where writers are occupied solely with the limits of the words before them; they are moments when they begin to write and to discover this site of potentiality as the source of all writing and as connected at all points throughout by the failure of their own words.

One could certainly describe this space as *interstitial*, as being always between two places—though these places are not really clearly defined either.[3] Or, one could describe it as "plastic," articulating something of the plasticity that characterizes the self always caught in-between more *static* ("reified") traditions and more *dynamic* ("fluid") experiences.[4] This state of constantly being in-between these two poles is what allows us to posit an "I" as that which lies in-between, but what also allows us to remain critical, when need be, of both traditions and our own personal and collective experiences. There is ultimately no need to rest secure on either foundation, but rather always to negotiate or interpret between these two sources of what identifies us.

It is, if I may venture to suggest it, also a spiritual space, the space of "unthinking" what has been thought. As the spiritual writer Mary Margaret Funk puts in terms parallel to Agamben's formulations of the pure potentiality of thought, it is the ability of the person to "prefer not to" do something[5]: "This unthinking process has wonderful benefits. There's a mind at ease that can either drink or not drink the coffee, and can eat either brown bread or a scone, with equal poise. The mind at peace is the beginning of *apatheia*, dispassion. Notice that this is not apathy but the full, conscious involvement of living from the center."[6] There is also a strict methodology at work here, one that recognizes how we must move fluidly between the theoretical and the practical, between the conceptual and the lived realities of the selves that we all always already are.

To provide but one example of what this might look like if fleshed out a bit, we might consider the writer's notebook, which, perhaps more often than not, lies blank. For each writer there is the hope of filling each notebook full of excellent writing. And yet there is also the reality that most notebooks will still, most likely, remain blank, staring back at the writer and asking them to fill its pages with words. The writer will try to fill them, of course, but they will never be as thought-provoking or as stimulating as one might wish them to be. Maybe this is all for the best, as they perhaps should remain blank, spurring the writer on by reminding them of just how empty they are and how truly vacant, as an author, we all are, or should be. It is the source, in fact, of one's creative potential *as* a writer.

There must be a certain horizon available to the writer that dictates how all of their writing is, in a certain sense, useless and unnecessary, itself completely contingent, much as Aquinas once saw that all he had written was "as straw." Everything one writes must be understood to have been written *on the precipice,* as it were, of a large chasm, as if it were merely about to tumble back into the abyss from which it had earlier come—an abyss, as we have seen, Agamben too is familiar with. And sometimes, beautifully, the works do fall right back into this abyss, and we should not want to stop them. In fact, we should perhaps hasten their withdrawal into one's own personal archive of errant thoughts and writings. If they did not do so, then we would have forgotten that "The pure potentiality of thought is a potentiality that is capable of not thinking, that is capable of not passing into actuality."[7]

The impulse to delve into one's potential, and to work with the infinitely undefined mass of possibilities that are there, has, of course, its practical implications: the "finished" product is not only *never* finished—I would go so far as to wager that it has less intrinsic value in and of itself for the person who created it than we might ever suspect. That is, it is designed first and foremost to have meaning *for* others, to convey a message to them, and therefore has, in a practical sense, far less meaning for the person who gave birth to it—or at least perhaps it should. Finding relish or seeking delight in the final publication is not the goal for the writer.

In terms of accessing this limitless potential, there must be *failure,* a multitude of projects begun and then abandoned, left to decay or ferment, I would only add, as *naturally* as possible. There is no shame in this process; rather, there must exist for each of us a pile of writing that has been abandoned and that is continuously part of the processes of being abandoned—that which can also, much later, perhaps, be mined for new thoughts or publications that are yet still able to spring from these oldest or darkest of our writings. We must learn to embrace such failed projects as part and parcel of the ones that do appear to stay a bit longer in the light (i.e., that are "published"), though even those works should be capable in some way of ultimately returning to the same abyss from which they came. Again, this process is, as Samuel Beckett once put it, one of learning to "fail better." Such failures, I would wager, are the only true representations we have before us.

There is a famous anecdote often conveyed concerning the actor Johnny Depp, how he never watches his own films. This oddity is something many point to as an elevation of the acting process which he feels himself committed to; he immerses himself within the process of acting to such a degree that the final product of the edited film is only a detraction from this larger experience. This story, I believe, would indicate something of the process of engaging with one's own potential that I am trying to isolate here for our inspection. We write to write, not to linger on the completed product, which is really little more than a way to get a job, social standing, or for another's benefit or edification. We certainly *do* write in order to reach out across the space between us and to change our social reality, but this is an aftereffect, and is not achieved by focusing on the final production of a finished product.

To formulate this in the terms I have pursued throughout this book, it is a journey toward what poet Seamus Heaney has called:

> The wideness of language, a journey where each point of arrival—whether in one's poetry or one's life—turned out to be a stepping stone rather than a destination, and it is that journey which has brought me now to this honoured spot. And yet the platform here feels more like a space station than a stepping stone, so that is why, for once in my life, I am permitting myself the luxury of walking on air.[8]

I like to think of this permanent state of never reaching the destination as part of the poet's location of being always already in "exile" from themselves—akin to Celan's desire for an encounter within a state of estrangement. And if the writer ever reaches such a spot as Heaney allowed himself to exist in, then this is a moment of "walking on air," and not something that roots us in our daily lives *as* writers.

Besides being the reality for many poets, whether self-imposed or forced upon them, this exilic living is—or should be—the theologian's task as well, which despite their firm rootedness in the scriptural realities of exile, they have largely neglected as a legitimate task. It is certainly also an explanation of what should not scare the theologian *within* the atheological—for even within this encounter with otherness, there is a hope of yet discovering ourselves *as* still theologians in some sense, though perhaps not the kind we had first envisioned ourselves being. Maybe if we think of exile as a permanent form of *poverty*, we might have a sense of what this could look like in reality—a theology of poverty as the poverty of theology—that which resists being called theology at all really, but which contains what may be the genuine heart of theological reflection. In this light, I expect many will be just as averse to the potential inside themselves and its ability to up-end one's representations of oneself, just as they are adverse to being poor in any literal or demonstrable sense. (And we might then begin at this point to understand why Alain Badiou's comment concerning Agamben is that his is a Franciscan ontology.) Power appears, to many, to be siphoned out of the recognition of one's poverty, though weakness may in fact turn out to be another form of strength, as Saint Paul himself noted many years ago.

The movement toward poverty is, therefore, not an inadvertent one, nor one made simply to give a thicker material description of what such an ex-ilic life might look like. To embrace poverty, weakness, or, in Jean Vanier's words, the process of "becoming little," we are forced to recognize an implicit and inherently ethical role taken up by the theologian, as by the poet in many ways (and, in the end, there may be little difference between them), for it is a role that recognizes the potential within oneself as a form of permanent otherness reflected by the many forms of otherness that exist outside of us. In the marginalized, oppressed, exiled, and abused others of society, we see *ourselves* too, and we must continue to stare deep into these faces, to look directly at their vulnerable precariousness, at their public exposure or "nudity," in order to comprehend something of the other-ness that we have deep within us, and which we often ignore or suppress.[9] Wanting to get in touch with an infinite source of potential within us, but refusing to see the otherness within us, is a recipe for perpetual deadlock (conveyed as the reality of writer's block for many).

The poverty of genius is not a game of waiting to become rich in order to initiate one's creativity, but to be responsible first with what one is given. It is an effort to subsist when no one is watching, in the poverty of one's own being, and without social recognition, which is to embrace one's po-tential insofar as it never seeks of its own accord to become rich or actual-ized in any substantial sense. This insight gives us a whole new sense of what writing is, or rather what it *can be*, far beyond the desire to be a best-selling writer.

There is, within this recognition as well, a specific "poverty of theology" that we should be attentive to as this form of inspiration likewise dictates the form (or formlessness) that a discipline itself can and should take. Theol-ogy, as a disciplinary effort (though, again, one could address poetry as well as a discipline that defies being a discipline at all really), could be seen as a perpetual *kenosis*, a pouring out of its supposed strength in order to embrace its weaknesses, and, thereby, the weaknesses of others within it. It, like every other representation, is a necessary failure that must reinvent itself at every turn. To grasp this is to grasp a spirituality understood as a form of relationship, and as such not simply as domains of self-knowledge or self-mastery—the traditionally strong senses that have wrongly, though often, been attached to theological study and writing. What we must seek to confront, then, is a sense of the loss of mastery of the subject, though not due to a lack of effort. We must gain a foreignness to ourselves that allows us to remain critical of ourselves and our efforts even in the midst of our greatest, apparent gains.

Acknowledgments

There are so many persons I would like to thank for their assistance and inspiration for this volume. I began working on the content while I was working in Leuven, Belgium, and completed the first draft in Chicago, though many ideas were formulated and revised in-between the two places. In this precarious balancing act between them, I was able to suture together some preliminary thoughts on poetry, the nature of representation, theology, and the art of writing. What is before you is my attempt to trace several lines of theological inquiry through both modern and contemporary philosophical interventions, and to give them concrete expression through the poetic arts and what this genre says on the nature of language.

I would like to thank the Faculty of Theology at the Katholieke Universiteit Leuven—especially Thomas Knieps, Johan Leemans, and Lieven Boeve—for their invitation to come speak to a gathering of graduate students in June 2013 on the topic of publishing in academia. There were many conversations afterward as well in which some of those in attendance encouraged me to develop my remarks further in the context of writing as a practice of spiritual formation. I was able to do just this upon receiving another invitation to speak to the Graduate Student Caucus at Loyola University Chicago in November of the same year. My thanks go out to Alyson Isaksson, Joseph Gulhaugen, Wendy Morrison, Silas Morgan, and the many great students, who make up the group and add so much to its vital dynamism, for their questions, comments, and warm embrace of the topic. The conclusion of the present text organically developed out of both talks.

The book as a whole has been expanded to point the way toward the conclusion, and it therefore brings together an explicit focus on poetics, representation and religious identity. Chapter 1 presents a revised and expanded version of an earlier essay—published as "The logic of the 'As If' and the Existence of God: An inquiry into the Nature of Belief in the Work of Jacques Derrida" (*Derrida Today* 4, no. 1 [2011]: 86–106)—and was intended to introduce the subject at hand within the context of deconstructivist thought and Jacques Derrida's own struggles to articulate his religious identity. Chapter 3 contains, but is not limited to, a revised and greatly expanded version of a much smaller essay on the work of Giorgio Agamben in relation to poetry published as "The Poetic Atheology of Giorgio Agamben: Defining the Scission between Poetry and Philosophy" (*Mosaic: A Journal for the Interdisciplinary Study of Literature* 45, no. 1 [2012]: 203–217).

My sincerest thanks are due to the many individuals in Leuven whose conversations greatly enriched the present work, including Stéphane Symons, Lieven Boeve, Frederiek Depoortere, Joeri Schrijvers, Joke Lambelin, and, especially, Kristien Justaert, whose encouragement on writing this volume, as well as the many conversations that led to it, was a great source of inspiration to me. My thanks are also due to Susan Ross, Hille Haker, John McCarthy, Mark Bosco, Aana Vigen, Edmondo Lupieri, Hanne Jacobs, and my many great colleagues here at Loyola University in Chicago who enriched the intellectual atmosphere around me greatly at the time I was completing this book.

A special word of thanks is also due to Joseph Gulhaugen, Jacob Torbeck, and Kathleen McNutt for the editorial assistance they have graciously provided for this book. And, as always, to Elisabeth and Rowan, whose own creative energies continue to give fuel to my own in ways I can hardly describe.

Finally, I am very grateful for permission to reprint lines from the following poems:

Paul Celan, "Go blind" and "Nocturnally Pouting" from *Poems of Paul Celan*, translated by Michael Hamburger. Copyright 1972, 1980, 1988, 1995 by Michael Hamburger. Reprinted with the permission of Persea Books, Inc.

Pamela Gillilan, "Write" from *All-Steel Traveller: New and Selected Poems*, Newcastle upon Tyne, UK: Bloodaxe, 1994. Reprinted with the permission of the Estate of Pamela Gillilan.

The lines from "An Atlas of the Difficult World" are from *An Atlas of the Difficult World: Poems 1988–1991* by Adrienne Rich. Copyright 1991 by Adrienne Rich. Used by permission of W. W. Norton & Company, Inc.

The lines from "Cartographies of Silence" are from *The Dream of a Common Language: Poems 1974–1977* by Adrienne Rich. Copyright 1978 by W. W. Norton & Company, Inc. Used by permission of W. W. Norton & Company, Inc.

The lines from "Diving into the Wreck" and from "Meditations for a Savage Child" are from *Diving into the Wreck: Poems 1971–1972* by Adrienne Rich. Copyright 1973 by W. W. Norton & Company, Inc. Used by permission of W. W. Norton & Company, Inc.

Wallace Stevens, "Not Ideas about the Thing but the Thing Itself" and "Study of Images II" from *The Collected Poems of Wallace Stevens* by Wallace Stevens. Copyright 1954 by Wallace Stevens, and copyright renewed 1982 by Holly Stevens. Used by permission of Alfred A. Knopf, an imprint of the Knopf Doubleday Publishing Group, a division of Penguin Random House LLC. All rights reserved.

Notes

Introduction

1. Celan, *Poems of Paul Celan*, 222–223. The German original reads:

ERBLINDE schon heut:
auch die Ewigkeit steht voller Augen—
darin
ertrinkt, was den Bildern hinweghalf
über den Weg, den sie kamen,
darin
erlischt, was auch dich aus der Sprache
fortnahm mit einer Geste,
die du geschehn ließt wie
den Tanz zweier Worte aus lauter
Herbst und Seide und Nichts.

2. For more on this quest within the context of the work of Giorgio Agamben, see my *Agamben and Theology*, chap. 1.

3. See my *Agamben and Theology* where the concept of potentiality plays a significant role throughout.

1. The Logic of the "As If" and the (Non)existence of God: An Inquiry into the Nature of Belief

1. Stevens, "Study of Images II," in *Collected Poetry and Prose*, 396.

2. Euripides, *Bacchae*, trans. G. S. Kirk.

3. Euripides, *Bacchae*, trans. G. S. Kirk, 53–54, lines 330–336 in the Greek text. Cf. the Seaford translation: Euripides, *Bacchae*, 85. My thanks are due to Clifton Kreps for his assistance with regard to locating this passage.

4. Segal, *Dionysiac Poetics and Euripides' Bacchae.*

5. Ibid., 286.

6. Ibid., 272–273.

7. Ibid., 340.

8. Pascal, *Pensées and Other Writings*, 152–158.

9. Kant, *Critique of Practical Reason*, quoted in Mary J. Gregor, *Practical Philosophy*, 241.

10. Kant, *Lectures on Logic*, 590–591.

11. Kant, *Critique of Pure Reason*, ed. and trans. Paul Guyer and Allen W. Wood, 525.

12. As concerns Kant's outlining of the "regulative principles" of thought, first, the mind must be assumed to be a "simple substance" that merges existence with personal identity, something that is not evident in and of itself through reason. Second, nature must be considered *as if* it were infinite in its inner and outer causes and without a first member though we are apt to make objects external to us into limited representations. Third, and "in regard to theology," we are told:

> [W]e have to consider everything that might ever belong to the context of possible experience as if this experience constituted an absolute unity, but one dependent through and through, and always still conditioned within the world of sense, yet at the same time as if the sum total of all appearances (the world of sense itself) had a single supreme and all-sufficient ground outside its range, namely an independent, original, and creative reason, as it were, in relation to which we direct every empirical use of our reason in its greatest extension as if the objects themselves had arisen from that original image of all reason. That means: it is not from a simple thinking substance that we derive the inner appearances of our soul, but from one another in accordance with the idea of a simple being; it is not from a highest intelligence that we derive the order of the world and its systematic unity, but rather it is from the idea of a most wise cause that we take the rule that reason is best off using for its own satisfaction when it connects up causes and effects in the world (Kant, *Critique of Pure Reason*, 607).

He continues by adding:

> [T]here is not the least thing to hinder us from assuming these ideas as objective and hypostatic, except only the cosmological ones, where reason runs up against an antinomy when it tries to bring this about (the psychological and theological ideas contain nothing of that sort at all). For there is no contradiction in them, so how could anyone dispute their objective reality, since he knows just as little about their possibility in denying it as we do in affirming it? (ibid.)

Yet, as he subsequently concludes, and as concerns the fundamental conjectural nature of Kant's positing of God's existence, "they should not be assumed in themselves, but their reality should hold only as that of a schema of the regulative principle for the systematic unity of all cognitions of nature; hence they should be grounded only as analogues of real things, but not as things in themselves" (ibid.).

13. Kant, *Critique of Pure Reason*, 609.

14. Ibid., 608.

15. See Vaihinger's response to Kant's ethics in 1911 entitled *Die Philosophie des Als Ob*, translated into English by C. K. Ogden as *The Philosophy of As If*. On the practical atheism allegedly at work in Kant's ethics based on an assumption of God, see Michalson Jr., *Kant and the Problem of God*.

16. Kearney, *Anatheism*, xvii.

17. Ibid., 15.

18. Ibid., 80, 180. See also Kearney, *God Who May Be*.

19. Kearney, *Anatheism*, 65. As Kearney renders it, "Unlike Benjamin and Levinas, therefore, Derrida's approach to the messianic hovers in the antechamber of messianism. He explores rather than embraces the anatheist option. His saving the Name does not entail a return to the Named. At best, it is an 'endless waiting in the desert.' A waiting for Godot who never comes" (65).

20. See Rothfield, *Kant After Derrida*.

21. See, among others, some exemplary uses of the "as if" (*comme si*) in Derrida's work, including "Before the Law" and "A Silkworm of One's Own," in *Acts of Religion*, 314, 383, 251; *Gift of Death*, 72–73; *Donner la mort*, 103–104; *Politics of Friendship*, 121, 149, 152; and *Politiques de l'amitié*, 142, 172, 175, in the context of Carl Schmitt and the friend/enemy distinction.

22. Weslati, "Aporias of the *As If*," in Rothfield, *Kant After Derrida*, 43–44.

23. This is not to suggest that the singularities of what claimed him were unimportant, or unessential; rather that Derrida more often chose to focus on the "impossible property" of any particularity, which is to say, as it approximates the universal concept he was dealing with, as, for example, in his alternation between his indebtedness to the French language and the structure of language itself. See Derrida, *Monolinguism of the Other*, 63–65, and *Le monolinguisme de l'autre*, 120–122.

24. Derrida, "Last of the Rogue States," 323–341. See also Derrida, *Rogues/ Voyous*.

25. Derrida, "Last of the Rogue States," 330.

26. Derrida, "Violence and Metaphysics: An Essay on the Thought of Emmanuel Levinas," in *Writing and Difference*, 153 / "Violence et métaphysique: Essai sur la pensée d'Emmanuel Levinas," in *L'écriture et la différence*, 227. Cf. his references to the history of representation and its Platonic legacy in "Envoi," in *Psyche*, 1:94–128 / "Envoi," in *Psyche*, 109–143.

27. See the recurring polarity (general/restricted, economic/aneconomic) within which all concepts are formed in Derrida's work. See Hurst, *Derrida Vis-à-vis Lacan*, 75.

28. See Derrida's appropriation of Levinas in Derrida, *Adieu*.

29. See Llewelyn, *Margins of Religion*; Shakespeare, *Derrida and Theology*; Hägglund, *Radical Atheism*; Bergo, Cohen, and Zagury-Orly, *Judeities/Judéités*; Sherwood and Hart, *Derrida and Religion*; Rayment-Pickard, *Impossible God*; Ofrat, *Jewish Derrida*; Hart, *Trespass of the Sign*.

30. See Lawlor, *This Is Not Sufficient*, 112–113.

31. Derrida, "Abraham, the Other," in *Judeities*, 13 / "Abraham, l'autre," in *Judéités*, 21–22. Cf. Derrida, "A Testimony Given," in Weber, *Questioning Judaism*, 41.

32. See Derrida, *Speech and Phenomena*, as well as his remarks in relation to Rousseau in *Of Grammatology*. See also Hobson, "The Logic of Representation," 53–69.

33. Derrida, "Abraham, the Other," 13 / "Abraham, l'autre," 22.

34. "The more radically you break with a certain dogmatism of the place or of the bond (communal, national, religious, of the state), the more you will be faithful to the hyperbolic, excessive demand, to the *hubris*, perhaps, of a universal and disproportionate responsibility toward the singularity of every other ('every other is wholly other' ['tout autre est tout autre']) is what I responded to Levinas one day, and I will perhaps say later what the hardly controllable stakes of this expression are, an expression that can barely be translated and is perhaps perverse)" (Derrida, "Abraham, the Other," 13 / "Abraham, l'autre," 22).

35. See Fritsch, *Promise of Memory*.

36. See Agamben, *Time That Remains*, 35–37.

37. See the remarks on the boundaries between animal and human made in Derrida, *Animal That Therefore I Am / L'animal que donc je suis*, as well as the role animality plays in relation to sovereignty in Derrida, *Beast and the Sovereign*, vol. 1 / *La bête et le souverain*.

38. See Derrida, "Différance," in *Margins of Philosophy*, 1–28 / "La Différance," in *Marges de la philosophie*, 1–29.

39. Derrida, "Abraham, the Other," 33 / "Abraham, l'autre," 40.

40. Ibid.

41. Ibid.

42. Ibid. 32/40.

43. Ibid.

44. See Hollander, "Is Deconstruction a Jewish Science?," 128–138.

45. Derrida, "As if I were Dead," in Brannigan, Robbins, and Wolfreys, *Applying: To Derrida*, 212–226.

46. The "suchness" of things that Derrida points toward is taken up perhaps nowhere more boldly than in the work of Agamben whose entire oeuvre, I would suggest, is directed toward the presentation (*not* representation) of a thing such as it is, or *as such*. Intending to flush out more fully the "whatever" nature of each thing over and against its limited representations, Agamben rather seeks to allow a thing's exposure to take place, to be in fact the taking place of everything. There henceforth develops a general overlap between his

comments on the presentation of a thing *as such* and the nature of paradigms which, according to him, strive to elevate this principle of respect for the singularity of an example above the dichotomous logic of division into particulars (a thing completely presented in its suchness) and universals (a thing reduced to its representation). A paradigm, rather, moves only from particulars to particulars, and thereby presenting the singularity of each thing instead of fostering its reductionist representations. Far from being coincidental to the scope of this chapter, Agamben concludes his discussion of paradigms with a description of a thing's suchness as exemplary given by Wallace Stevens: "It is possible that to seem—it is to be, / As the sun is something seeming and it is. / The sun is an example. What it seems / It is / and in such seeming all things are" (Stevens, "Description Without Place," in *Collected Poetry and Prose*, 296). See Agamben, "What Is a Paradigm?," in *Signature of All Things*, 32.

47. Derrida, "Epoché and Faith," in Sherwood and Hart, *Derrida and Religion*, 33.

48. See how these themes are dealt with in Derrida, *Memoires*. As these lectures were originally delivered in English translation by Derrida, there is no original French text to cite in this regard.

49. Ibid., 160.

50. See Derrida, *Work of Mourning / Chaque fois unique*.

51. Derrida, *Sovereignties in Question*, 103. On "hauntology," see also Derrida, *Specters of Marx*.

52. Derrida, *On the Name*, 55–56 / *Sauf le nom*, 55–56.

53. Derrida, *Sovereignties in Question*, 120–122. See also, Agamben, "What Is the Contemporary?," in *What Is an Apparatus?*, 1–24.

54. Derrida, *Sovereignties in Question*, 169.

55. Note the manner in which this poetic theme is flushed out more fully in relation to philosophical reflection in Critchley, *Things Merely Are*.

56. See Derrida, "Circumfessions," in Bennington, *Jacques Derrida*, 70. See also the manner in which Derrida's views on iterability affect the presentation of literature in Szafraniec, *Beckett, Derrida, and the Event of Literature*.

57. See Derrida, "Envoi," in *Psyche*, 1:94–128.

58. Gillilan, *All-Steel Traveller*, 104.

2. Aesthetics among the Metaphysical Ruins: The Poetry of Paul Celan Seen through the Works of Jacques Derrida and Philippe Lacoue-Labarthe

1. This fracture I am referring to can be located in the definition of beauty as a lawfulness yet without a law, a state that gives rise to an interminable state of interpretive judgment. See Kant, *Critique of the Power of Judgment*.

2. See the wonderful manner in which Judith Butler speaks about the failures of subjective representation in her *Giving an Account of Oneself*, as well as in her more recent *Frames of War*.

3. We might note, for example, the way that Paul Ricoeur, in *Rule of Metaphor*, deals with the construction of meaning amid the tensions between the historical and the metaphorical.

4. On this legacy of enjambment, see Agamben, *End of the Poem*.

5. Lauterwein, *Anselm Kiefer, Paul Celan*.

6. Celan, "Nocturnally Pouting," in *Poems of Paul Celan*, 61.

7. See Ross, *Aesthetic Paths of Philosophy*, as well as the work of Jean-Luc Marion, to name but one example of such a conjunction. See also Marion, *Being Given*. His conceptualization of the "saturated phenomenon" is merged in his work with a certain understanding of mysticism; see his introduction to Kessler and Sheppard, *Mystics*.

8. For more on this aspect of Derrida's work, see my *Between the Canon and the Messiah*.

9. I have elaborated on this in "The Logic of the 'As If' and the Existence of God," 86–106.

10. See Derrida, *Beast and the Sovereign*, vol. 1 / *La bête et le souverain*.

11. Derrida, "How to Avoid Speaking: Denials," 147 / "Comment ne pas parler: Dénégations," 550. Kevin Hart, for one, has utilized the notion of negative theology in relation to Derrida's work in his *Trespass of the Sign*. For an essay attempting to critique Hart's tendency to read Derrida's work as a "general negative theology," see Ware, "Impossible Passions," 171–183. On this theme, see also Coward and Foshay, *Derrida and Negative Theology*.

12. Derrida, "How to Avoid Speaking: Denials," 166 / "Comment ne pas parler: Dénégations," 561.

13. See ibid., 156 / 550. See also, his remarks on animality in general in Derrida, *The Animal That Therefore I Am / L'animal que donc je suis*, as well as Lawlor, *This Is Not Sufficient*.

14. See Derrida, *Aporias*, 40–41 / *Apories*, 77–78.

15. See Derrida's critique of the archaeological method in his *Archive Fever*.

16. Derrida, *Aporias*, 72–73 / *Apories*, 128.

17. Derrida, *Sauf le nom*, 36. On the concept of messianicity, see Derrida, *Specters of Marx*.

18. Derrida, *Aporias*, 78 / *Apories*, 137, emphasis in the original.

19. See Derrida, *Rogues*, 144 / *Voyous*, 198–199. On the Kantian legacy in Derrida's thought, see also Rothfield, *Kant After Derrida*.

20. See Derrida, *Sauf le nom*, 54.

21. See also van der Heiden, "The Poetic Experience of Language and the Task of Thinking: Derrida on Celan," 115–125. For an interpretation of Derrida in relation to the poetry of Wallace Stevens, see Miller, "Anachronistic Reading," 75–91.

22. Agamben, *Kingdom and the Glory*.

23. Derrida, *Beast and the Sovereign*, 1:231 / *La bête et le souverain*, 308. Cf. Derrida's remarks on majesty and sovereignty as they run throughout his study on freedom and democracy in *Rogues / Voyous*.

24. See his initial essays in Derrida, *Writing and Difference / L'écriture et la différence.*

25. Derrida, *Sovereignties in Question*, 95.

26. See Derrida, "How to Avoid Speaking," 156 / "Comment ne pas parler," 550, and "Passions: 'An Oblique Offering,'" in *On the Name*, 24–25. In the latter essay, he goes on to add that secrets are neither sacred nor profane, neither involved in a "learned ignorance" (negative theology) nor an esoteric doctrine (mysticism) (26). See also, his remarks on the "secret" in a series of interviews geared toward this thematic in Derrida and Ferraris, *A Taste for the Secret*, especially 58–59.

27. Derrida, *Sovereignties in Question*, 96.

28. On the merger of theology and poetics into a theopoetics, see the initial work of Wilder, *TheoPoetic*, as well as its recent usage in the writings of Kearney, *Anatheism*, and Caputo, *The Weakness of God*.

29. See, in particular, Rich, *Diving into the Wreck*, and Stevens, *Collected Poetry and Prose*. On Derrida distinguishing himself from the work of Agamben, see his remarks on Agamben in *Beast and the Sovereign*, vol. 1 / *La bête et le souverain*. On his proximity and yet distance from Lacoue-Labarthe, see his introduction to Lacoue-Labarthe's *Typology*, 1–42.

30. See Derrida, *Beast and the Sovereign*, 1:267 / *La bête et le souverain*, 358.

31. Ibid., 1:260 / 350. Malek Moazzam-Doulat, for example, has suggested that Derrida's messianism actually serves to reveal a god who must either hide or recede and is therefore not sovereign. See Moazzam-Doulat, "Future Impossible," 73–81.

32. This same "double division" which Derrida speaks of is developed in much further detail, and in a somewhat parallel register by Agamben in his *Time That Remains*. Despite Agamben's insistence that his approach is in stark contrast to Derrida's, their mutual illumination of the poetic in regard to sovereignty strikes a similar chord on this point. There is a good deal more that could be said on the matter, especially concerning Derrida's apparent contentions with the alleged archaeologists—Freud, Foucault, and Agamben—insofar as his critique of each (that they claim to locate an "origin," or a presence) is really very similar to his own elaboration of the division of division itself that indicates a showing only through the failures of representation. If one reads this in conjunction with Agamben's own establishment of a position wherein the only genuine representation is one that fails to represent the "thing itself," given alongside his own utilization of a Pauline "division of division itself," we might have cause to reformulate the very stakes of this philosophical debate.

33. Derrida, *Beast and the Sovereign*, 1:271–272 / *La bête et le souverain*, 364–365.

34. See Celan, *Atemwende*.

35. See Derrida, "Envoi," in *Psyche*, 1:127. See also his remarks on a possible "preorigin" in his essay "Khōra," in *On the Name*, 126.

36. Derrida, *Beast and the Sovereign*, 1:273 / *La bête et le souverain*, 366.

37. Ibid., 1:230 / 307.

38. Lacoue-Labarthe, *Poetry as Experience*, 13 / *La poésie comme expérience*, 23. See also the excellent study of the work of Lacoue-Labarthe in Martis, *Philippe Lacoue-Labarthe*.

39. Lacoue-Labarthe, *Poetry as Experience*, 15 / *La poésie comme expérience*, 27.

40. Ibid., 43 / 63. Cf. Hans-Georg Gadamer, *Gadamer on Celan*.

41. See how such experiences are depicted in John Felstiner's excellent biography of Celan, *Paul Celan*.

42. Lacoue-Labarthe, *Poetry as Experience*, 32–33 / *La poésie comme expérience*, 50.

43. Ibid., 48 / 71.

44. Ibid., 60 / 90.

45. See, for example, how this term is discussed in Hurst, *Derrida Vis-à-vis Lacan*.

46. For more on these themes in Ricoeur's work, see chapter 4 of my *Between the Canon and the Messiah*.

47. Lacoue-Labarthe, *Poetry as Experience*, 60 / *La poésie comme expérience*, 90.

48. See Ricoeur, *Oneself as Another*.

49. Lacoue-Labarthe, *Poetry as Experience*, 65 / *La poésie comme expérience*, 96.

50. Such a portrayal of "natural time" interrupting our historical representations runs throughout much of Walter Benjamin's work, as well as Agamben's. See, notably, Agamben, *Time That Remains*, as well as Fenves, *Messianic Reduction*.

51. Ibid., 41 / 61.

52. Ibid., 112–113 / 155.

53. Ibid., 50–51 / 75.

54. Ibid., 54 / 81.

55. Ibid.

56. See Ibid., 67 / 99.

57. See Ibid., 68 / 100.

58. For more on such a hypothesis in the context of the poetic, as we have been following thus far, see Critchley, *Things Merely Are*.

59. See Lacoue-Labarthe, *Poetry as Experience*, 73–79 / *La poésie comme expérience*, 106–114. See also Agamben, *Open*.

60. Lacoue-Labarthe, *Poetry as Experience*, 84–86 / *La poésie comme expérience*, 119–122.

61. See Ibid., 113 / 156–157.

62. Something like this is sensed and noted in Bruno Latour's more recent writings on religion as a focus on what is immanently present to us, and in contrast to scientific methods which attempt to deal with what is "transcendent." See Latour, *Rejoicing*.

63. Such efforts have been mirrored recently by Judith Butler and her attempt to show how presentation can only come about through the cracks of failed representations. See Butler, *Frames of War*.

64. Celan, *Breathturn*, 250–251.

65. See Kant, *Lectures on Logic*, 590–591; see also Kant, *Critique of Pure Reason*, 525. Kant's work subsequently influenced Hans Vaihinger, whose response to Kant's ethics in 1911 was entitled *The Philosophy of As If: A System of the Theoretical, Practical, and Religious Fictions of Mankind*.

66. See Agamben, "The Thing Itself," in *Potentialities*, 27–38. See also, on the "thing itself" and its relation to metaphor and representation, Bigger, *Between* Chora *and the* Good.

67. Note how this push beyond language is determined as a site of our potential "infancy" according to Agamben. See Agamben, *Infancy and History*.

68. Rich, "Diving into the Wreck," in *Diving into the Wreck*, 23–24.

69. See Rich, "The Burning of Paper Instead of Children," in *Will to Change*, 15–18. On Rich's relationship to language in general, see Hedley, "Surviving to Speak New Language," 40–62.

70. Rich, "An Atlas of the Difficult World," in *An Atlas of the Difficult World*, 4.

71. Rich, "Meditations for a Savage Child," in *Diving into the Wreck*, 55–56.

72. Ibid., 58. On Agamben's concept of infancy, see his *Infancy and History*.

73. I elaborate a good deal on the tension between Agamben and Derrida in chapter 2 of my *Between the Canon and the Messiah*.

74. Rich, " 'Rotted Names,' " in *What Is Found There*, 202. See also Estrin, "Space-Off and Voice-Over," 23–46.

75. All poems can be found in Stevens, *Collected Poetry and Prose*.

76. Stevens, "Not Ideas About the Thing but the Thing Itself," in *Collected Poetry and Prose*, 451–452.

77. Ibid., 452.

78. Critchley. *Things Merely Are*, 10.

79. Lacoue-Labarthe, *Poetry as Experience*, 50–51. See also, what is perhaps the only critical study available at present on the work of Lacoue-Labarthe, Martis, *Philippe Lacoue-Labarthe*, as well as Ross, *Aesthetic Paths of Philosophy*.

80. Derrida, *Monolinguism of the Other*.

81. Rilke, *Duino Elegies and The Sonnets to Orpheus*.

82. Rich, "Cartographies of Silence," in *Dream of a Common Language*, 16–20. This same impulse can be seen on display in her series of poems entitled "Contradictions: Tracking Poems," in *Your Native Land, Your Life*, 83–112.

3. On Language and Its Profanation: Beyond Representation in the Poetic Theory of Giorgio Agamben

1. Agamben, *End of the Poem*, 30.

2. Ibid., 38.

3. For more on Agamben's relation to Dante, see chapter 1 of my *Agamben and Theology*.

4. Agamben, *End of the Poem*, 39.

5. Ibid., 41 (set in italics in the original).

6. Pinsky, *Democracy, Culture and the Voice of Poetry*, 47.

7. Agamben, *End of the Poem*, 36–37.

8. Ibid., 37.

9. See, in fact, recent publications within his *Homo Sacer* series (all published by Stanford University Press).

10. Agamben, *End of the Poem*, 66.

11. Ibid., 66.

12. Ibid., 67.

13. See the central thesis of Agamben, *Sacrament of Language*.

14. Agamben, *End of the Poem*, 67.

15. See the treatment given to this topic in Agamben, *Language and Death*.

16. Agamben, *End of the Poem*, 63.

17. Ibid., 64. Cf. his parallel remarks in Agamben, *Language and Death*, 33–34.

18. Agamben, *End of the Poem*, 65.

19. See Agamben, *Coming Community*, as well as his *Idea of Prose*.

20. Agamben, *End of the Poem*, 79.

21. Agamben, *Language and Death*, 77.

22. Ibid.

23. Ibid., 78.

24. Ibid., 30.

25. Agamben, *End of the Poem*, 68–71.

26. See Agamben, *Potentialities*, 177–184.

27. Agamben, *End of the Poem*, 67. As he will later explicate, "In entering into *grammata* in being written, the animal voice is separated from nature, which is inarticulate and cannot be written; it shows itself in letters as a pure intention to signify whose signification is unknown (it is in this respect similar to *glossolalia* and Augustine's *vocabulum emortuum*)" (ibid., 69).

28. Ibid., 70, emphasis in the original. And, Agamben adds: "The experience of this 'crossing over,' which constitutes the site of Pascoli's poetic dictation, is an experience of death. It is only in dying that the animal voice is, in the letter, destined to enter signifying language as pure intention to signify; and it is only in dying that articulated language can return to the indistinct womb of the voice from which it originated. Poetry is the experience of the letter, but the letter has its place in death: in the death of the voice (onomatopoeia) or the death of language (*glossolalia*) the two of which coincide in the brief flash of *grammata*" (ibid., 71).

29. This is followed shortly thereafter with the comment, "Here the pure language of names, in which the dead voice is inscribed, decays and cannot be separated from the glossolalia of words that 'veil and darken their meaning'"

(Agamben, *End of the Poem*, 71). Hence, I would suggest, the prominence given in Pascoli's poetry to proper names, those words without a proper signification, "being simply a reference of the linguistic code to itself" (ibid., 70).

30. Benjamin, "On the Concept of History," in *Selected Writings*, vol. 4; Agamben, *Man without Content*, 104–115.

31. Agamben, *Infancy and History*, 16.

32. Ibid., 17.

33. Ibid., 47.

34. Agamben, "What Is the Contemporary?," in *What Is an Apparatus?*, 42.

35. Agamben, *Infancy and History*, 16.

36. Ibid., 26.

37. Ibid., 49.

38. Agamben, *Man without Content*, 107; Durantaye, *Giorgio Agamben*, 46–48.

39. Agamben, *Infancy and History*, 49.

40. Such a distinction, it could be noted, can be seen prominently on display in the contrast between Baudelaire's *Paris Spleen,* with its clamor for a distance taken from the mystical and which yet almost manages to restore it through its intoxicated rhythms, and Rilke's *Notebooks of Malte Laurids Brigge,* with its lamentation upon the lost divine and yet its long meditation upon what has been regained through our efforts to construct ourselves in writing (cf. Agamben, *Remnants of Auschwitz*, 61–62).

41. Agamben, *Coming Community*, 89–105.

42. See Agamben, *Open.*

43. Agamben, *Infancy and History*, 49.

44. Heidegger, *Being and Time.*

45. Cunningham, "On the Line," 121–122; Lacoue-Labarthe, *Poetry as Experience / La poésie comme experience.*

46. Agamben, *Infancy and History*, 49.

47. See his remarks on Dante and language in Agamben, *End of the Poem*, 124–125.

48. Agamben, *Stanzas*, xvii.

49. Ibid.

50. Agamben, *Idea of Prose*, 97–98.

51. Agamben, *Remnants of Auschwitz*, 38–39; Durantaye, *Giorgio Agamben,* 260–262.

52. Plato, *Republic*, 607b–c.

53. Agamben, *Stanzas*, xvi.

54. Ibid.

55. Ibid.

56. Agamben, *Language and Death*, 74.

57. Ibid., 74.

58. See Agamben, *Idea of Prose.*

59. See Agamben, *Language and Death*, 78.

60. Agamben, *End of the Poem*, 79.

61. Agamben, *Remnants of Auschwitz*.

62. Agamben, *Language and Death*, 30.

63. Ibid., 78–81.

64. Ibid., 30.

65. See Benjamin, "On Language as Such and on the Language of Man."

66. Agamben, *End of the Poem*, 77.

67. See Agamben, *Kingdom and the Glory*, and his *Sacrament of Language*.

68. Durantaye, *Giorgio Agamben*, 58–76, 141, 280.

69. See Agamben, *Man without Content*.

70. Agamben, *End of the Poem*, 77.

71. See also my "Canon as an Act of Creation: Giorgio Agamben and the Extended Logic of the Messianic," 132–158.

72. Agamben, *End of the Poem*, 78; cf. Colebrook, "Agamben," 107–120.

73. See Agamben, *Profanations*.

74. Agamben, *Time That Remains*, 87; cf. Kaufman, "The Saturday of Messianic Time," 37–54.

75. See also Stewart, "Rhyme and Freedom."

76. Agamben, *Man without Content*, 100.

77. Ibid., 101.

78. Ibid.

79. Agamben, *Profanations*, 59; Agamben, *Infancy and History*, 37.

80. T. S. Eliot, "The Hollow Man," in *Poems, 1909–1925*, 77–82.

81. Agamben, *Stanzas*, 50–51.

82. Agamben, *End of the Poem*, 90–91.

83. Ibid., 91.

84. See Agamben, *Homo Sacer*.

85. Vogt, "S/Citing the Camp," 100; cf. Agamben, *Remnants of Auschwitz*.

86. Agamben, *End of the Poem*, 91.

87. Ibid., 90; see also Caproni, *Wall of the Earth*.

88. See Agamben, *Time That Remains*, 87.

89. See Agamben, *End of the Poem*, 91–92.

90. Agamben, *End of the Poem*, 90.

91. See the essays on "potentiality" gathered in Agamben, *Potentialities*. Agamben's appropriation of Caproni's work is not without its inherent distortions, of course. Cf. Colilli, "The Theological Materials of Modernity (On Giorgio Agamben)," 465–479.

92. For more on this concept, see my *Agamben and Theology*.

93. Bartoloni, *Interstitial Writing*, 73.

94. Cf. the concept of "sovereignty" as developed in Agamben, *State of Exception*.

95. See Agamben, *Coming Community*, 1–2.

96. Agamben, *Potentialities*, 253.

97. Stevens, *Opus Posthumous*, 106.

98. Adorno, "An Essay on Cultural Criticism and Society," in *Prisms*, 34

99. Adorno, *Negative Dialectics*, 362.

100. See Downey, "Zones of Indistinction," 109–125.

101. Heidegger. "What Are Poets For?," 142.

102. Lacoue-Labarthe, *Poetry as Experience*, 75.

103. See Agamben on Deleuzian immanence in *Potentialities*, 220–239.

104. Agamben, *End of the Poem*, 93.

105. Ibid.

106. Ibid.

107. Watkin, *Literary Agamben*, 193.

108. Agamben, *End of the Poem*, 94.

109. See ibid., 101.

110. See Agamben, *Language and Death*, 104–106.

111. As quoted in Agamben, *Potentialities*, 115.

112. See Agamben, *Time That Remains*.

113. Agamben, *Potentialities*, 115.

114. Bartoloni, *Interstitial Writing*, 71.

115. On Celan's poetry in relation to Agamben, see Moore's " 'Speak, You Also: Encircling Trauma," 87–99.

116. Agamben, *Idea of Prose*, 44.

117. Ibid., 107.

118. Agamben, "What Is the Contemporary?," in *What Is an Apparatus? and Other Essays*, 42.

119. Stevens, *Opus Posthumous*.

120. Agamben, "What Is the Contemporary?," in *What Is an Apparatus? and Other Essays*, 52.

121. See Agamben, *Time That Remains*.

122. Agamben, *End of the Poem*, 114.

123. Ibid., 114.

124. Ibid., 115.

125. See Agamben, *Coming Community*; on the motif of the face within an ethical paradigm, see Agamben, *Means without End*. Agamben's use of the "face" as an ethical construct remains an unacknowledged debt to Levinas in his work that Agamben has not yet directly addressed as such.

Conclusion: The Spiritual and Creative Failures of Representation, or On the Art of Writing

1. Caputo, *Insistence of God*, 261.

2. Agamben, *Potentialities*, 184.

3. See Bartoloni, *Interstitial Writing*.

4. Malabou, *Plasticity at the Dusk of Writing*, 81.

5. See Agamben's essay "Bartleby, or On Contingency," in his *Potentialities*, 243–271.

6. Funk, *Humility Matters*, 18.

7. Agamben, *Potentialities*, 215.

8. Heaney, "Crediting Poetry: The Nobel Lecture," in *Opened Ground*, 449.

9. I am thinking here of the convergence of two lines of related thought: Agamben, *Nudities*, and Butler, *Precarious Life*.

Bibliography

Adorno, Theodor W. "An Essay on Cultural Criticism and Society." In *Prisms*, 17–34. Translated by Samuel and Shierry Weber. Cambridge, MA: MIT Press, 1967.

———. *Negative Dialectics*. Translated by E. B. Ashton. London: Continuum, 1973.

Agamben, Giorgio. *The Coming Community*. Translated by Michael Hardt. Minneapolis: University of Minnesota Press, 1993.

———. *The End of the Poem: Studies in Poetics*. Translated by Daniel Heller-Roazen. Stanford, CA: Stanford University Press, 1999.

———. *Homo Sacer: Sovereign Power and Bare Life*. Translated by Daniel Heller-Roazen. Stanford, CA: Stanford University Press, 1998.

———. *The Idea of Prose*. Translated by Michael Sullivan and Sam Whitsitt. Albany: State University of New York Press, 1995.

———. *Infancy and History: On the Destruction of Experience*. Translated by Liz Heron. London: Verso, 1993.

———. *The Kingdom and the Glory: For a Theological Genealogy of Economy and Government*. Translated by Lorenzo Chiesa and Matteo Mandarini. Stanford, CA: Stanford University Press, 2011.

———. *Language and Death: The Place of Negativity*. Translated by Karen E. Pinkus and Michael Hardt. Minneapolis: University of Minnesota Press, 1991.

———. *The Man without Content*. Translated by Georgia Albert. Stanford, CA: Stanford University Press, 1999.

———. *Nudities*. Translated by David Kishik and Stefan Pedatella. Stanford, CA: Stanford University Press, 2010.

———. *The Open: Man and Animal*. Translated by Kevin Attell. Stanford, CA: Stanford University Press, 2004.

———. *Potentialities: Collected Essays in Philosophy*. Translated by Daniel Heller-Roazen. Stanford, CA: Stanford University Press, 2000.

———. *Profanations*. Translated by Jeff Fort. New York: Zone, 2007.

———. *Remnants of Auschwitz: The Witness and the Archive*. Translated by Daniel Heller-Roazen. New York: Zone, 2002.

———. *The Sacrament of Language*. Translated by Adam Kotsko. Stanford, CA: Stanford University Press, 2010.

———. *The Signature of All Things: On Method*. Translated by Luca D'Isanto and Kevin Attell. New York: Zone, 2009.

———. *Stanzas: Word and Phantasm in Western Culture*. Translated by Ronald L. Martinez. Minneapolis: University of Minnesota Press, 1993.

———. *State of Exception. Homo Sacer II.1*. Translated by Kevin Attell. Chicago: University of Chicago Press, 2005.

———. *The Time That Remains: A Commentary on the Letter to the Romans*. Translated by Patricia Dailey. Stanford, CA: Stanford University Press, 2005.

———. *What Is an Apparatus? And Other Essays*. Translated by David Kishik and Stefan Pedatella. Stanford, CA: Stanford University Press, 2009.

Bartoloni, Paolo. *Interstitial Writing: Calvino, Caproni, Sereni and Svevo*. Market Harborough, UK: Troubador, 2003.

Baudelaire, Charles. *Paris Spleen*. Translated by Louise Varèse. New York: New Directions Publication Corporation, 1970.

Benjamin, Walter. "On Language as Such and on the Language of Man." In *Selected Writings*, vol. 1, edited by Marcus Bullock and Michael W. Jennings and translated by Edmund Jephcott et al., 62–74. Cambridge, MA: Harvard University Press, 1996.

———. "On the Concept of History." In *Selected Writings*, vol. 4, edited by Howard Eiland and Michael W. Jennings and translated by Edmund Jephcott et al., 389–400. Cambridge, MA: Harvard University Press, 2003.

Bergo, Bettina, Joseph Cohen, and Raphael Zagury-Orly, eds. *Judeities: Questions for Jacques Derrida*. Translated by Bettina Bergo and Michael B. Smith. New York: Fordham University Press, 2007.

Bigger, Charles P. *Between* Chora *and the* Good: *Metaphor's Metaphysical Neighborhood*. New York: Fordham University Press, 2005.

Butler, Judith. *Frames of War: When Is Life Grievable?* London: Verso, 2009.

———. *Giving an Account of Oneself*. New York: Fordham University Press, 2005.

———. *Precarious Life: The Powers of Mourning and Violence*. London: Verso, 2004.

Caproni, Giorgio. *The Wall of the Earth*. Translated by Pasquale Verdicchio. Montreal: Guernica, 1992.

Caputo, John. *Insistence of God: A Theology of Perhaps*. Bloomington: Indiana University Press, 2013.

———. *The Weakness of God: A Theology of the Event.* Bloomington: Indiana University Press, 2006.

Celan, Paul. *Atemwende: Vorstufen, Textgenese, Endfassung.* Frankfurt a. M.: Suhrkamp, 2000.

———. *Breathturn.* Translated by Pierre Joris. Copenhagen: Green Integer, 2006.

———. *Poems of Paul Celan.* Translated by Michael Hamburger. New York: Persea, 1972.

Colebrook, Claire. "Agamben: Aesthetics, Potentiality, and Life." *South Atlantic Quarterly* 107, no. 1 (2008): 107–120.

Colilli, Paul. "The Theological Materials of Modernity (On Giorgio Agamben)." *Italica* 85, no. 4 (2008): 465–479.

Coward, Harold, and Toby Foshay, eds. *Derrida and Negative Theology.* Albany: State University of New York Press, 1992.

Critchley, Simon. *Things Merely Are: Philosophy in the Poetry of Wallace Stevens.* London: Routledge, 2005.

Cunningham, Conor. "On the Line: Martin Heidegger and Paul Celan." *Genealogy of Nihilism.* London: Routledge, 2002.

Derrida, Jacques. "Abraham, l'autre." In *Judéités: Questions pour Jacques Derrida,* edited by Joseph Cohen and Raphael Zagury-Orly, 11–42 Paris: Galilée, 2003.

———. "Abraham, the Other." In *Judeities: Questions for Jacques Derrida,* edited by Bettina Bergo, Joseph Cohen, and Raphael Zagury-Orly, and translated by Bettina Bergo and Michael B. Smith, 1–35. New York: Fordham University Press, 2007.

———. *Acts of Religion.* Edited by Gil Anidjar. Translated by Mary Quaintance. London: Routledge, 2002.

———, *Adieu: To Emmanuel Levinas.* Translated by Pascale-Anne Brault and Michael Naas. Stanford, CA: Stanford University Press, 1996.

———. *The Animal That Therefore I Am.* Edited by Marie-Louise Mallet. Translated by David Wills. New York: Fordham University Press, 2008.

———. *Aporias: Dying-Awaiting (One Another at) the "Limits of Truth."* Translated by Thomas Dutoit. Stanford, CA: Stanford University Press, 1993.

———. *Apories: mourir—s'attendre aux 'limites de la verite.'* Paris: Galilée, 1996.

———. *Archive Fever: A Freudian Impression.* Translated by Eric Prenowitz. Chicago: University of Chicago Press, 1996.

———. "As If I Were Dead: An Interview with Jacques Derrida." In *Applying: To Derrida,* edited by John Brannigan, Ruth Robbins, and Julian Wolfreys, 212–226. London: Macmillan, 1996.

———. *The Beast and the Sovereign.* Vol. 1. Edited by Michel Lisse, Marie-Louise Mallet, and Ginette Michaud. Translated by Geoffrey Bennington. Chicago: University of Chicago Press, 2009.

————. *Chaque fois unique, la fin du monde*. Edited by Pascale-Anne Brault and Michael Naas. Paris: Galilée, 2003.

————. "Circumfessions." In *Jacques Derrida*, edited and translated by Geoffrey Bennington, 3–315. Chicago: University of Chicago Press, 1996.

————. "Comment ne pas parler: Dénégations." In *Psyché: Inventions de l'autre*, 145–200.

————. *Donner la mort*. Paris: Galilée, 1999.

————. "Epoché and Faith: An Interview with Jacques Derrida." In *Derrida and Religion: Other Testaments*, edited by Yvonne Sherwood and Kevin Hart, 27–50. New York: Routledge, 2005.

————. *The Gift of Death*. Translated by David Wills. Chicago: University of Chicago Press, 1995.

————. "How to Avoid Speaking: Denials." In *Psyche: Inventions of the Other*, 2:143–196.

————. "The Last of the Rogue States: The 'Democracy to Come,' Opening in Two Turns." *South Atlantic Quarterly* 103 (2004): 323–341.

————. *L'animal que donc je suis*. Paris: Galilée, 2006.

————. *L'écriture et la différence*. Paris: Éditions du Seuil, 1979.

————. *La bête et le souverain*. Paris: Galilée, 2008–2010.

————. *Le monolinguisme de l'autre, ou la prothèse d'origine*. Paris: Galilée, 1996.

————. *Marges de la philosophie*. Paris: Minuit, 1972.

————. *Margins of Philosophy*. Translated by Alan Bass. Chicago: University of Chicago Press, 1982.

————. *Memoires: For Paul de Man*. New York: Columbia University Press, 1989.

————. *Monolinguism of the Other, or, The Prosthesis of Origin*. Translated by Patrick Mensah. Stanford, CA: Stanford University Press, 1998.

————. *Of Grammatology*. Translated by Gayatri Chakravorty Spivak. Baltimore, MD: Johns Hopkins University Press, 1978.

————. *On the Name*. Edited by Thomas Dutoit. Translated by David Wood, John P. Leavey Jr., and Ian McLeod. Stanford, CA: Stanford University Press, 1995.

————. *The Politics of Friendship*. Translated by George Collins. London: Verso, 1997.

————. *Politiques de l'amitié: suivi de L'oreille de Heidegger*. Paris: Galilée, 1994.

————. *Psyché: Inventions de l'autre*. Paris: Galilée, 1987.

————. *Psyche: Inventions of the Other*. Vol. 1. Edited by Peggy Kamuf and Elizabeth Rottenberg. Stanford, CA: Stanford University Press, 2007.

————. *Psyche: Inventions of the Other*. Vol. 2. Edited by Peggy Kamuf and Elizabeth Rottenberg. Stanford, CA: Stanford University Press, 2008.

————. *Rogues: Two Essays on Reason*. Translated by Pascale-Anne Brault and Michael Naas. Stanford, CA: Stanford University Press, 2004.

————. *Sauf le nom.* Paris: Galilée, 1993.

————. *Sovereignties in Question: The Poetics of Paul Celan.* Edited by Thomas Dutoit and Outi Pasanen. New York: Fordham University Press, 2005.

————. *Specters of Marx: The State of the Debt, the Work of Mourning and the New International.* London, Routledge, 2006.

————. *Speech and Phenomena, and Other Essays on Husserl's Theory of Signs.* Translated by David B. Allison. Evanston, IL: Northwestern University Press, 1973.

————. "A Testimony Given." In *Questioning Judaism: Interviews by Elisabeth Weber,* translated by Rachel Bowlby, 39–58 Stanford, CA: Stanford University Press, 2004.

————. *Voyous: Deux essais sur la raison.* Paris: Galilee, 2003.

————. *The Work of Mourning.* Translated by Pascale-Anne Brault and Michael Naas. Chicago: Chicago University Press, 2003.

————. *Writing and Difference.* Translated by Alan Bass. Chicago: University of Chicago Press, 1978.

Derrida, Jacques, and Maurizio Ferraris. *A Taste for the Secret.* Edited by Giacomo Donis and David Webb. Translated by Giacomo Donis. Cambridge: Polity, 2001.

Dickinson, Colby. *Agamben and Theology.* London: T&T Clark, 2011.

————. *Between the Canon and the Messiah: The Structure of Faith in Contemporary Continental Thought.* London: Continuum, 2013.

————. "Canon as an Act of Creation: Giorgio Agamben and the Extended Logic of the Messianic." *Bijdragen* 71, no. 2 (2010): 132–158.

————. "The Logic of the 'As If' and the Existence of God: An inquiry into the Nature of Belief in the Work of Jacques Derrida." *Derrida Today* 4, no. 1 (2011): 86–106.

Downey, Andrew. "Zones of Indistinction: Giorgio Agamben's 'Bare Life' and the Politics of Aesthetics." *Third Text* 23, no. 2 (2009): 109–125.

Durantaye, Leland de la. *Giorgio Agamben: A Critical Introduction.* Stanford, CA: Stanford University Press, 2009.

Eliot, T. S. *Poems, 1909–1925.* London: Faber and Faber, 1933.

Estrin, Barbara L. "Space-Off and Voice-Over." *Women's Studies* 25, no. 1 (1995): 23–46.

Euripides. *The Bacchae.* Translated by G. S. Kirk. Cambridge: Cambridge University Press, 1979.

————. *Bacchae.* Translated by Richard Seaford. Warminster: Aris & Philips, 1996.

Felstiner, John. *Paul Celan: Poet, Survivor, Jew.* New Haven, CT: Yale University Press, 1995.

Fenves, Peter. *The Messianic Reduction: Walter Benjamin and the Shape of Time.* Stanford, CA: Stanford University Press, 2010.

Fritsch, Matthias. *The Promise of Memory: History and Politics in Marx, Benjamin, and Derrida.* Albany: State University of New York Press, 2005.

Funk, Mary Margaret. *Humility Matters: Toward Purity of Heart*. Collegeville, MN: Liturgical Press, 2013.

Gadamer, Hans-Georg. *Gadamer on Celan: "Who Am I and Who Are You?" and Other Essays*. Translated by Richard Heinemann and Bruce Krajewski. Albany: State University of New York Press, 1997.

Gillilan, Pamela. *All-Steel Traveller: New and Selected Poems*. Newcastle upon Tyne, UK: Bloodaxe, 1994.

Gregor, Mary J., ed. *Practical Philosophy*. Cambridge: Cambridge University Press, 1996.

Hägglund, Martin. *Radical Atheism: Derrida and the Time of Life*. Stanford, CA: Stanford University Press, 2008.

Hart, Kevin. *The Trespass of the Sign: Deconstruction, Theology and Philosophy*. Cambridge: Cambridge University Press, 1989.

Heaney, Seamus. *Opened Ground: Poems 1966–1996*. London: Faber and Faber, 2001.

Hedley, Jane. "Surviving to Speak New Language: Mary Daly and Adrienne Rich." *Hypatia* 7, no. 2 (1992): 40–62.

Heidegger, Martin. *Being and Time*. Translated by Joan Stambaugh. Albany: State University of New York, 1996.

———. "What Are Poets For?" In *Poetry, Language, Thought*, translated by Albert Hofstadter, 91–142. New York: Harper, 1971.

Hobson, Marian. "The Logic of Representation (and the Representation of Logic)." *parallax* 10, no. 3 (2004): 53–69.

Hollander, Dana. "Is Deconstruction a Jewish Science? Reflections on 'Jewish Philosophy' in Light of Jacques Derrida's *Judéïtés*." *Philosophy Today* 50, no. 1 (2006): 128–38.

Hurst, Andrea. *Derrida Vis-à-vis Lacan: Interweaving Deconstruction and Psychoanalysis*. New York: Fordham University Press, 2008.

Kant, Immanuel. *Critique of Practical Reason*. In *Practical Philosophy*, edited and translated by Mary J. Gregor, 133–271. Cambridge: Cambridge University Press, 1996.

———. *Critique of Pure Reason*. Edited and translated by Paul Guyer and Allen W. Wood. Cambridge: Cambridge University Press, 1997.

———. *Critique of the Power of Judgment*. Cambridge: Cambridge University Press, 2000.

———. *Lectures on Logic*. Translated by J. Michael Young. Cambridge: Cambridge University Press, 2004.

Kaufman, Eleanor. "The Saturday of Messianic Time (Agamben and Badiou on the Apostle Paul)." *South Atlantic Quarterly* 107, no. 1 (2008): 37–54.

Kearney, Richard. *Anatheism: Returning to God After God*. New York: Columbia University Press, 2010.

———. *The God Who May Be: A Hermeneutics of Religion*. Indianapolis, IN: Indiana University Press, 2001.

Kessler, Michael, and Christian Sheppard, eds. *Mystics: Presence and Aporia.* Chicago: University of Chicago Press, 2003.

Lacoue-Labarthe, Phillippe. *La poésie comme experience.* Paris: C. Bourgois, 1986.

———. *Poetry as Experience.* Translated by Andrea Tarnowski. Stanford, CA: Stanford University Press, 1999.

———. *Typography: Mimesis, Philosophy, Politics.* Translated by Christopher Fynsk. Stanford, CA: Stanford University Press, 1998.

Latour, Bruno. *Rejoicing: On the Torments of Religious Speech.* Translated by Julie Rose. Cambridge: Polity, 2013.

Lauterwein, Andrea. *Anselm Kiefer, Paul Celan: Myth, Mourning and Memory.* Translated by David H. Wilson. London: Thames and Hudson, 2007.

Lawlor, Leonard. *This Is Not Sufficient: An Essay on Animality and Human Nature in Derrida.* New York: Columbia University Press, 2007.

Llewelyn, John. *Margins of Religion: Between Kierkegaard and Derrida.* Bloomington: Indiana University Press, 2009.

Malabou, Catherine. *Plasticity at the Dusk of Writing: Dialectic, Destruction, Deconstruction.* Translated by Carolyn Shread. New York: Columbia University Press, 2010.

Marion, Jean-Luc. *Being Given: Toward a Phenomenology of Givenness.* Translated by Jeffrey Kosky. Stanford, CA: Stanford University Press, 2002.

Martis, John. *Philippe Lacoue-Labarthe: Representation and the Loss of the Subject.* New York: Fordham University Press, 2005.

Michalson, Gordon, Jr. *Kant and the Problem of God.* Malden, Mass.: Blackwell, 1999.

Miller, J. Hillis. "Anachronistic Reading." *Derrida Today* 3, no. 1 (2010): 75–91.

Moazzam-Doulat, Malek. "Future Impossible: Carl Schmitt, Jacques Derrida, and the Problem of Political Messianism." *Philosophy Today* 52, no. 1 (2008): 73–81.

Moore, Isabel A. "'Speak, You Also': Encircling Trauma." *Journal for Cultural Research* 9, no. 1 (2005): 87–99.

Ofrat, Gideon. *The Jewish Derrida.* Translated by Peretz Kidron. Syracuse, NY: Syracuse University Press, 2001.

Pascal, Blaise. *Pensées and Other Writings.* Edited by Anthony Levi. Translated by Honor Levi. Oxford: Oxford University Press, 2008.

Pinsky, Robert. *Democracy, Culture and the Voice of Poetry.* Princeton, NJ: Princeton University Press, 2002.

Plato. *The Republic.* Edited by G. R. F. Ferrari. Translated by Tom Griffith. Cambridge: Cambridge University Press, 2000.

Rayment-Pickard, Hugh. *Impossible God: Derrida's Theology.* Aldershot, UK: Ashgate, 2003.

Rich, Adrienne. "An Atlas of the Difficult World." In *An Atlas of the Difficult World: Poems 1988–1991,* 3–28. New York: W. W. Norton, 1991.

————. "The Burning of Paper Instead of Children." In *The Will to Change: Poems 1968–1970*, 15–18. New York: W. W. Norton, 1971.

————. "Cartographies of Silence." In *The Dream of a Common Language: Poems 1974–1977*, 16–20. New York: W. W. Norton, 1978.

————. "Contradictions: Tracking Poems." In *Your Native Land, Your Life*, 83–112. New York: W. W. Norton, 1986.

————. *Diving into the Wreck: Poems 1971–1972*. New York: W. W. Norton, 1973.

————. "Rotted Names." In *What Is Found There: Notebooks on Poetry and Politics*, 197–205. New York: W. W. Norton, 2003.

Ricoeur, Paul. *Oneself as Another*. Translated Kathleen Blamey. Chicago: University of Chicago Press, 1995.

————. *The Rule of Metaphor: The Creation of Meaning in Language*. Translated by Robert Czerny, Kathleen McLaughlin, and John Costello. London: Routledge, 1977.

Rilke, Rainer Maria. *Duino Elegies and The Sonnets to Orpheus*. Translated by Stephen Mitchell. New York: Vintage, 1982.

Ross, Alison. *Aesthetic Paths of Philosophy: Presentation in Kant, Heidegger, Lacoue-Labarthe, and Nancy*. Stanford, CA: Stanford University Press, 2007.

Rothfield, Phil, ed. *Kant after Derrida*. Manchester: Clinamen Press, 2002.

Segal, Charles. *Dionysiac Poetics and Euripides' Bacchae*. Princeton: Princeton University Press, 1982.

Shakespeare, Steven. *Derrida and Theology*. London: Continuum, 2009.

Sherwood, Yvonne, and Kevin Hart, eds. *Derrida and Religion: Other Testaments*. London: Routledge, 2005.

Stewart, Susan. "Rhyme and Freedom." In *The Sound of Poetry, The Poetry of Sound*, edited by Marjorie Derloff and Craig Dworkin, 29–48. Chicago: University of Chicago Press, 2009.

Stevens, Wallace. *Collected Poetry and Prose*. New York: Library of America, 1997.

————. *Opus Posthumous: Poems, Plays, Prose*. New York: Vintage, 1990.

Szafraniec, Asja. *Beckett, Derrida, and the Event of Literature*. Stanford, CA: Stanford University Press, 2007.

Vaihinger, Hans. *Die Philosophie des Als Ob: System der theoretischen, praktischen und religiösen Fiktionen der Menschheit auf Grund eines idealistischen Positivismus*. Berlin: Reuther und Reichard, 1911.

————. *The Philosophy of As If: A System of the Theoretical, Practical, and Religious Fictions of Mankind*. Translated by C. K. Ogden. London: Routledge, 1965.

van der Heiden, Gert-Jan. "The Poetic Experience of Language and the Task of Thinking: Derrida on Celan." *Philosophy Today* 53, no. 2 (2009): 115–125.

Vogt, Erik. "S/Citing the Camp." In *Politics, Metaphysics, and Death: Essays on Giorgio Agamben's Homo Sacer*, edited by Andrew Norris, 74–106. Durham, NC: Duke University Press, 2005.

Ware, Owen. "Impossible Passions: Derrida and Negative Theology." *Philosophy Today* 49, no. 2 (2005): 171–183.

Watkin, William. *Literary Agamben: Adventures in Logopoeisis*. London: Continuum, 2010.

Weslati, Hager. "Aporias of the *As If*: Derrida's Kant and the Question of Experience." In *Kant after Derrida*, edited by Phil Rothfield, 18–49 Manchester: Clinamen Press, 2002.

Wilder, Amos Niven. *TheoPoetic: Theology and the Religious Imagination*. Philadelphia: Fortress, 1976.

Index

Perspectives in Continental Philosophy
John D. Caputo, series editor

John D. Caputo, ed., *Deconstruction in a Nutshell: A Conversation with Jacques Derrida.*

Michael Strawser, *Both/And: Reading Kierkegaard—From Irony to Edification.*

Michael D. Barber, *Ethical Hermeneutics: Rationality in Enrique Dussel's Philosophy of Liberation.*

James H. Olthuis, ed., *Knowing Other-wise: Philosophy at the Threshold of Spirituality.*

James Swindal, *Reflection Revisited: Jürgen Habermas's Discursive Theory of Truth.*

Richard Kearney, *Poetics of Imagining: Modern and Postmodern.* Second edition.

Thomas W. Busch, *Circulating Being: From Embodiment to Incorporation—Essays on Late Existentialism.*

Edith Wyschogrod, *Emmanuel Levinas: The Problem of Ethical Metaphysics.* Second edition.

Francis J. Ambrosio, ed., *The Question of Christian Philosophy Today.*

Jeffrey Bloechl, ed., *The Face of the Other and the Trace of God: Essays on the Philosophy of Emmanuel Levinas.*

Ilse N. Bulhof and Laurens ten Kate, eds., *Flight of the Gods: Philosophical Perspectives on Negative Theology.*

Trish Glazebrook, *Heidegger's Philosophy of Science.*

Kevin Hart, *The Trespass of the Sign: Deconstruction, Theology, and Philosophy.*

Mark C. Taylor, *Journeys to Selfhood: Hegel and Kierkegaard.* Second edition.

Dominique Janicaud, Jean-François Courtine, Jean-Louis Chrétien, Michel Henry, Jean-Luc Marion, and Paul Ricoeur, *Phenomenology and the "Theological Turn": The French Debate.*

Karl Jaspers, *The Question of German Guilt*. Introduction by Joseph W. Koterski, S.J.

Jean-Luc Marion, *The Idol and Distance: Five Studies*. Translated with an introduction by Thomas A. Carlson.

Jeffrey Dudiak, *The Intrigue of Ethics: A Reading of the Idea of Discourse in the Thought of Emmanuel Levinas*.

Robyn Horner, *Rethinking God as Gift: Marion, Derrida, and the Limits of Phenomenology*.

Mark Dooley, *The Politics of Exodus: Søren Kierkegaard's Ethics of Responsibility*.

Merold Westphal, *Overcoming Onto-Theology: Toward a Postmodern Christian Faith*.

Edith Wyschogrod, Jean-Joseph Goux, and Eric Boynton, eds., *The Enigma of Gift and Sacrifice*.

Stanislas Breton, *The Word and the Cross*. Translated with an introduction by Jacquelyn Porter.

Jean-Luc Marion, *Prolegomena to Charity*. Translated by Stephen E. Lewis.

Peter H. Spader, *Scheler's Ethical Personalism: Its Logic, Development, and Promise*.

Jean-Louis Chrétien, *The Unforgettable and the Unhoped For*. Translated by Jeffrey Bloechl.

Don Cupitt, *Is Nothing Sacred? The Non-Realist Philosophy of Religion: Selected Essays*.

Jean-Luc Marion, *In Excess: Studies of Saturated Phenomena*. Translated by Robyn Horner and Vincent Berraud.

Phillip Goodchild, *Rethinking Philosophy of Religion: Approaches from Continental Philosophy*.

William J. Richardson, S.J., *Heidegger: Through Phenomenology to Thought*.

Jeffrey Andrew Barash, *Martin Heidegger and the Problem of Historical Meaning*.

Jean-Louis Chrétien, *Hand to Hand: Listening to the Work of Art*. Translated by Stephen E. Lewis.

Jean-Louis Chrétien, *The Call and the Response*. Translated with an introduction by Anne Davenport.

D. C. Schindler, *Han Urs von Balthasar and the Dramatic Structure of Truth: A Philosophical Investigation*.

Julian Wolfreys, ed., *Thinking Difference: Critics in Conversation*.

Allen Scult, *Being Jewish/Reading Heidegger: An Ontological Encounter*.

Richard Kearney, *Debates in Continental Philosophy: Conversations with Contemporary Thinkers*.

Jennifer Anna Gosetti-Ferencei, *Heidegger, Hölderlin, and the Subject of Poetic Language: Toward a New Poetics of Dasein*.

Jolita Pons, *Stealing a Gift: Kierkegaard's Pseudonyms and the Bible*.

Jean-Yves Lacoste, *Experience and the Absolute: Disputed Questions on the Humanity of Man*. Translated by Mark Raftery-Skehan.

Charles P. Bigger, *Between* Chora *and the Good: Metaphor's Metaphysical Neighborhood.*

Dominique Janicaud, *Phenomenology "Wide Open": After the French Debate.* Translated by Charles N. Cabral.

Ian Leask and Eoin Cassidy, eds., *Givenness and God: Questions of Jean-Luc Marion.*

Jacques Derrida, *Sovereignties in Question: The Poetics of Paul Celan.* Edited by Thomas Dutoit and Outi Pasanen.

William Desmond, *Is There a Sabbath for Thought? Between Religion and Philosophy.*

Bruce Ellis Benson and Norman Wirzba, eds., *The Phenomenology of Prayer.*

S. Clark Buckner and Matthew Statler, eds., *Styles of Piety: Practicing Philosophy after the Death of God.*

Kevin Hart and Barbara Wall, eds., *The Experience of God: A Postmodern Response.*

John Panteleimon Manoussakis, *After God: Richard Kearney and the Religious Turn in Continental Philosophy.*

John Martis, *Philippe Lacoue-Labarthe: Representation and the Loss of the Subject.*

Jean-Luc Nancy, *The Ground of the Image.*

Edith Wyschogrod, *Crossover Queries: Dwelling with Negatives, Embodying Philosophy's Others.*

Gerald Bruns, *On the Anarchy of Poetry and Philosophy: A Guide for the Unruly.*

Brian Treanor, *Aspects of Alterity: Levinas, Marcel, and the Contemporary Debate.*

Simon Morgan Wortham, *Counter-Institutions: Jacques Derrida and the Question of the University.*

Leonard Lawlor, *The Implications of Immanence: Toward a New Concept of Life.*

Clayton Crockett, *Interstices of the Sublime: Theology and Psychoanalytic Theory.*

Bettina Bergo, Joseph Cohen, and Raphael Zagury-Orly, eds., *Judeities: Questions for Jacques Derrida.* Translated by Bettina Bergo and Michael B. Smith.

Jean-Luc Marion, *On the Ego and on God: Further Cartesian Questions.* Translated by Christina M. Gschwandtner.

Jean-Luc Nancy, *Philosophical Chronicles.* Translated by Franson Manjali.

Jean-Luc Nancy, *Dis-Enclosure: The Deconstruction of Christianity.* Translated by Bettina Bergo, Gabriel Malenfant, and Michael B. Smith.

Andrea Hurst, *Derrida Vis-à-vis Lacan: Interweaving Deconstruction and Psychoanalysis.*

Jean-Luc Nancy, *Noli me tangere: On the Raising of the Body.* Translated by Sarah Clift, Pascale-Anne Brault, and Michael Naas.

Jacques Derrida, *The Animal That Therefore I Am.* Edited by Marie-Louise Mallet, translated by David Wills.

Jean-Luc Marion, *The Visible and the Revealed.* Translated by Christina M. Gschwandtner and others.

Michel Henry, *Material Phenomenology.* Translated by Scott Davidson.

Jean-Luc Nancy, *Corpus*. Translated by Richard A. Rand.

Joshua Kates, *Fielding Derrida*.

Michael Naas, *Derrida From Now On*.

Shannon Sullivan and Dennis J. Schmidt, eds., *Difficulties of Ethical Life*.

Catherine Malabou, *What Should We Do with Our Brain?* Translated by Sebastian Rand, Introduction by Marc Jeannerod.

Claude Romano, *Event and World*. Translated by Shane Mackinlay.

Vanessa Lemm, *Nietzsche's Animal Philosophy: Culture, Politics, and the Animality of the Human Being*.

B. Keith Putt, ed., *Gazing Through a Prism Darkly: Reflections on Merold Westphal's Hermeneutical Epistemology*.

Eric Boynton and Martin Kavka, eds., *Saintly Influence: Edith Wyschogrod and the Possibilities of Philosophy of Religion*.

Shane Mackinlay, *Interpreting Excess: Jean-Luc Marion, Saturated Phenomena, and Hermeneutics*.

Kevin Hart and Michael A. Signer, eds., *The Exorbitant: Emmanuel Levinas Between Jews and Christians*.

Bruce Ellis Benson and Norman Wirzba, eds., *Words of Life: New Theological Turns in French Phenomenology*.

William Robert, *Trials: Of Antigone and Jesus*.

Brian Treanor and Henry Isaac Venema, eds., *A Passion for the Possible: Thinking with Paul Ricoeur*.

Kas Saghafi, *Apparitions—Of Derrida's Other*.

Nick Mansfield, *The God Who Deconstructs Himself: Sovereignty and Subjectivity Between Freud, Bataille, and Derrida*.

Don Ihde, *Heidegger's Technologies: Postphenomenological Perspectives*.

Suzi Adams, *Castoriadis's Ontology: Being and Creation*.

Richard Kearney and Kascha Semonovitch, eds., *Phenomenologies of the Stranger: Between Hostility and Hospitality*.

Michael Naas, *Miracle and Machine: Jacques Derrida and the Two Sources of Religion, Science, and the Media*.

Alena Alexandrova, Ignaas Devisch, Laurens ten Kate, and Aukje van Rooden, *Re-treating Religion: Deconstructing Christianity with Jean-Luc Nancy*. Preamble by Jean-Luc Nancy.

Emmanuel Falque, *The Metamorphosis of Finitude: An Essay on Birth and Resurrection*. Translated by George Hughes.

Scott M. Campbell, *The Early Heidegger's Philosophy of Life: Facticity, Being, and Language*.

Françoise Dastur, *How Are We to Confront Death? An Introduction to Philosophy*. Translated by Robert Vallier. Foreword by David Farrell Krell.

Christina M. Gschwandtner, *Postmodern Apologetics? Arguments for God in Contemporary Philosophy*.

Ben Morgan, *On Becoming God: Late Medieval Mysticism and the Modern Western Self*.

Neal DeRoo, *Futurity in Phenomenology: Promise and Method in Husserl, Levinas, and Derrida.*

Sarah LaChance Adams and Caroline R. Lundquist, eds., *Coming to Life: Philosophies of Pregnancy, Childbirth, and Mothering.*

Thomas Claviez, ed., *The Conditions of Hospitality: Ethics, Politics, and Aesthetics on the Threshold of the Possible.*

Roland Faber and Jeremy Fackenthal, eds., *Theopoetic Folds: Philosophizing Multifariousness.*

Jean-Luc Marion, *The Essential Writings.* Edited by Kevin Hart.

Adam S. Miller, *Speculative Grace: Bruno Latour and Object-Oriented Theology.* Foreword by Levi R. Bryant.

Jean-Luc Nancy, *Corpus II: Writings on Sexuality.*

David Nowell Smith, *Sounding/Silence: Martin Heidegger at the Limits of Poetics.*

Gregory C. Stallings, Manuel Asensi, and Carl Good, eds., *Material Spirit: Religion and Literature Intranscendent.*

Claude Romano, *Event and Time.* Translated by Stephen E. Lewis.

Frank Chouraqui, *Ambiguity and the Absolute: Nietzsche and Merleau-Ponty on the Question of Truth.*

Noëlle Vahanian, *The Rebellious No: Variations on a Secular Theology of Language.*

Michael Naas, *The End of the World and Other Teachable Moments: Jacques Derrida's Final Seminar.*

Jean-Louis Chrétien, *Under the Gaze of the Bible.* Translated by John Marson Dunaway.

Edward Baring and Peter E. Gordon, eds., *The Trace of God: Derrida and Religion.*

Vanessa Lemm, ed., *Nietzsche and the Becoming of Life.*

Aaron T. Looney, *Vladimir Jankélévitch: The Time of Forgiveness.*

Richard Kearney and Brian Treanor, eds., *Carnal Hermeneutics.*

Tarek R. Dika and W. Chris Hackett, *Quiet Powers of the Possible: Interviews in Contemporary French Phenomenology.* Foreword by Richard Kearney.

Jeremy Biles and Kent L. Brintnall, eds., *Georges Bataille and the Study of Religion.*

William S. Allen, *Aesthetics of Negativity: Blanchot, Adorno, and Autonomy.*

Don Ihde, *Husserl's Missing Technologies.*

Colby Dickinson and Stéphane Symons, eds., *Walter Benjamin and Theology.*

Emmanuel Falque, *Crossing the Rubicon: The Borderlands of Philosophy and Theology.* Translated by Reuben Shank. Introduction by Matthew Farley.

Emmanuel Falque, *The Wedding Feast of the Lamb: Eros, the Body, and the Eucharist.* Translated by George Hughes.

Colby Dickinson, *Words Fail: Theology, Poetry, and the Challenge of Representation.*

Jean Wahl, *Transcendence and the Concrete: Selected Writings.* Edited and with an Introduction by Alan D. Schrift and Ian Alexander Moore.

An Yountae, *The Decolonial Abyss: Mysticism and Cosmopolitics from the Ruins.*

CPSIA information can be obtained
at www.ICGtesting.com
Printed in the USA
BVOW00s2207071216

470023BV00001B/25/P